In the Spirit

of friendship. Best Wishes for
a great year. I hope this
brings some positive insight
into life.
Always,
Leslie

In the Spirit

the inspirational writings of

Susan L. Taylor

HarperPerennial

A Division of HarperCollins*Publishers*

Designed by Maryam Marne Zafar

Library of Congress Cataloging-in-Publication Data
Taylor, Susan L.
   In the spirit : the inspirational writings of Susan L. Taylor. — 1st ed.
     p.   cm.
   Originally published: New York : Amistad, c1993.
   ISBN 0-06-097645-4 (pbk.)
   1. Spiritual life. I. Title.
  [BL624.T395 1994]
   291.4´3—dc20   94-29608

94 95 96 97 98 HC 10 9 8 7 6 5 4 3 2 1

DEDICATION

For Mommy and Daddy,
for their parents and grands,
for the ancestors who kept the faith,
who willed themselves to live
and paved our way.

And for Shana-Nequai, and the next generation.

Acknowledgements

I am grateful

To my beloved husband and friend, Khephra Burns, who is always there; to my sister, Lillian Baker, for loving and counseling me.

To writer DorisJean Austin, whose love and guidance helped give birth to this book; editor Malaika Adero, who early on envisioned it; literary agent Marie Brown for her guidance; economist and journalist Lena Sherrod for encouraging and critiquing the work; Derryale Barnes for inputting and polishing the manuscript.

To *Essence* editors Stephanie Stokes Oliver and Valerie Wilson Wesley for their wisdom and advice and Charlotte Wiggers for her editing expertise; to my coworkers Michelle Webb, Debra Parker and Sherrill Clarke and to Ellin LaVar for their dedication and support; and to LaVon Leak-Wilks for her assistance on the cover design.

To my life-supporting womenfriends, who push and pull me through: Pat Martin, Pat Ramsay, Peggy Ruffin, Terrie Williams, Roxanna Bilal, Ruth Sanchez-Laviera, Andriette Earl-Bozeman and Attallah Shabazz.

To *Essence* cofounders Ed Lewis and Clarence Smith for their faith in me; to my friend and predecessor Marcia Ann Gillespie; to the editorial team and my beloved *Essence* family, past and present.

To Eric Butterworth, whose Sunday sermons give me insight and strength.

CONTENTS

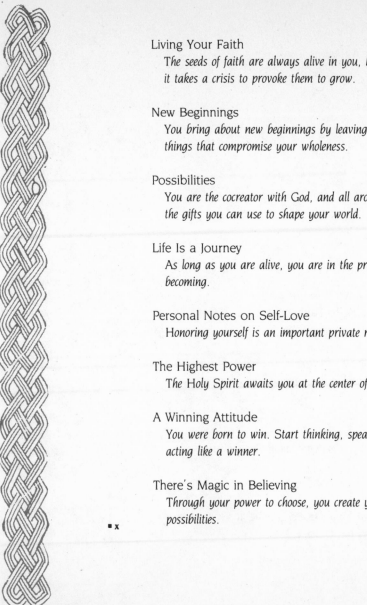

Preface

Often I'm asked where I get my ideas for In the Spirit, my monthly editorial in *Essence* magazine, and if I ever have difficulty finding something to write about. I write about what I'm challenged by, what I might be struggling through and trying to awaken within myself. And because every day comes with a new trial, there is always something new to discover.

The book *In the Spirit* contains new essays, some previously published ones that have been expanded, and a few of my and our readers' favorites. All of the essays return to the same truth: that by cultivating a deep inner awareness, we develop the wisdom and faith necessary to create happy and fulfilling lives. *In the Spirit* explores the potential of divinity within each of us and tells how we can begin to trust it enough to do the work critical to our survival, so that we will walk by faith and not by sight alone.

In creating *In the Spirit*, I have drawn on inspirational teachings from rich and diverse sources. And I've been blessed to discover an essential singular and universal truth: that God *is*.

In the Spirit is a deeply personal book. It's about my healing and yours. It contains the seeds I want to plant in our hearts and within our universal garden so that we can uplift our people and ease the suffering in our world.

Introduction
Coming to Faith

That day of transformation seems so long ago.
It was a cold, rainy Sunday morning in November, and I
was having difficulty breathing. I'd been short of breath
for several days and had awakened that morning with a
pain in my chest. It felt as though a heavy weight were
pressing against my heart. I thought I was having a heart
attack. I called and asked my baby's father to come get
her and take me to the hospital for a chest X-ray.

So many things seemed to be happening at once. I was
24 years old, newly separated and living on my own with
my year-old daughter, Shana-Nequai. I'd been hired, for
$500 a month, as a freelance beauty editor at the new
magazine *Essence*. Money was tight: The monthly rent on
my new apartment was $368, and I had car payments,
utilities bills and other living expenses to cover.

I had been worrying a lot: My car was broken, my rent
was due, the holidays were just around the corner, and I
had $3 in my wallet and no backup in the bank. That past
summer I had started a new company, Nequai Cosmetics,
which was doing well, but I had lost my business because
the inventory was in my husband's beauty salon, and I
had no safe way to get it out.

That memorable Sunday I sat in the emergency room
with people who, like me, had no health insurance and

had been waiting for hours to be examined, tested and given some relief. My mood brightened when the young physician assured me that I wasn't dying; my heart seemed fine and he could detect no medical problems. But he did say that I seemed overly anxious and needed to relax.

But how could I relax when the earth was shifting under my feet? This was no *little* funk I was in. I felt depressed and hopeless. I couldn't imagine any bright tomorrows. I had been working hard since high school, had saved my money and built my company, and suddenly I had nothing to show for it. When I left my volatile marriage, I went from middle-class wife to poor single mother overnight.

It was late afternoon when I finally left the hospital and stepped into the crisp fall air. It had stopped raining, and I decided to walk home, from Manhattan to The Bronx. I needed to save the carfare and use the time to think.

I was feeling so alone. I had no money, no man. All my troubles were on my mind: How was I going to feed my baby? Pay the rent? Did I really even *want* to make it through the night? I was gripped by fear.

As I was walking up Broadway, I passed a church, and something drew me through the big brass doors into the evening service. A powerful force was guiding me. I hadn't been to church in years, and I had been raised always to "dress" to go to worship. But there I was sitting in a back pew wearing jeans and a leather jacket.

That night I heard a sermon that would change my life. The preacher said that our minds could change our world. That no matter what our troubles, if we could put them aside for a moment, focus on possible solutions and imagine a joyous future, we would find a peace within, and positive experiences would begin to unfold.

I had grown up Catholic and had gone to Catholic schools. I had read my catechism each day and attended church seven days a week at times. I believed that God was in heaven, that there was power in the statues of the saints, in the cross that hung in the center of the church, in the wafer placed on my tongue when I took communion. I thought the nuns and the priest had a direct line to God. Never once had I heard that there was power within *me*.

The minister's talk about the power of positive thinking and looking within for peace and solutions seemed simplistic, rather like hocus-pocus. But I was clinging to the edge, not sure I even had the will to hold on. What did I have to lose?

I decided to try it. I gathered up some of the small pamphlets in the church vestibule. Little did I know I was taking the first step toward replacing my fears with faith. I was breaking a negative cycle that had so engulfed me that I couldn't see life's beauty. It was the beginning of my realization that our thoughts create our reality.

I felt lighter as I headed home over the bridge that crosses the Harlem River. I felt that tremendous weight lifting from my heart. All the next week I worked to keep my commitment to try to think positively. Instead of mourning the things that I felt were missing in my life—happiness, my new business, a love relationship—I began counting my many blessings. Throughout the day I would pause and give thanks for my life—for breath and health and the fact that I was here. I thanked God for my

healthy child, for the part-time job that was keeping a roof over our heads. I gave thanks that I still had my mother and my good friends.

Within days I forgot that I'd been depressed. The shortness of breath and pressure in my chest disappeared. And within weeks I was offered another part-time job, teaching at Ophelia DeVore's modeling school. Several months later, Marcia Ann Gillespie became editor-in-chief of *Essence* and offered me a full-time position as the fashion and beauty editor, and my salary doubled. I began to see clearly how focusing on my blessings instead of my woes increased the many good things in my life.

My positive thoughts, prayers and affirmations didn't cause God to treat me more kindly and make changes in my life. Rather, the positive, life-affirming thoughts and words changed me. They lifted my faith. Now I was focused on the beauty of life, on my talents and strengths—on the power of God within me. I began to step into the world expecting good things to happen. I was learning that, depending on my positive or negative energy, I have the power to attract either good or bad things.

The wisdom of the minister's words is still unfolding for me: Having faith means being active, not sitting back bemoaning life and waiting for a change to come. It means loving ourselves, believing in ourselves and using the transforming power of God to move our lives forward. The Reverend Alfred Miller's words were simple. The truth is always simple, but living it is not easy.

If I'd had a man or felt any sweetness in my life that Sunday morning, I would have lingered in bed. If not for the pain in my chest, I wouldn't have gone to the hospital. If I'd had money, I would have taken a taxi or gotten my car repaired and driven past that church as I had many a Sunday. I would have missed that important sermon. I might have missed renewing my life.

During these difficult times, the most revolutionary thing we can do is to have faith—to hold a positive vision of what we want for ourselves and for our children and to put the energy behind that vision and make it a reality. Our enemy is not the system or those who foster it. Our enemy. is fear—fear that blinds us to truth, fear that keeps us ensnarled in anger and disempowered by grief. Fear keeps us focused on what we don't want rather than on what we need to lead us toward a harmonious, healthful way of living.

With faith we are never alone. We realize that we have within us everything we need to overcome any of life's challenges. There have been countless times since that Sunday when I have felt the earth shake beneath me. This is what is happening to our people today, and to people throughout the world. It's but one of the many ways in which the Holy Spirit speaks to us and encourages us to make changes. At times it seems as if our face must hit the ground before we listen, before we heed our inner wisdom.

We are a spiritual people. I have faith that these hard times are awakening us to a new unity and a reaffirmation of purpose. Faith played a large part in the lives of our elders—and that should tell us something. Their faith sustained them. We must never become too sophisticated to believe. Our parents and grandparents were

strong women and men, sensitive and sensible. Despite the many forces arrayed against them, they moved the race forward. They took us higher. Faith gave them the inner security to know that they would find their way, even when they couldn't see the light. Keeping the faith is part of our legacy. We are a people who created astronomy, mathematics, medicine. We created art, built empires. We have suffered dispersion and barbaric oppression. We have endured and survived. We have come too far not to go the distance.

Let us continue to be champions of faith, not just when it's easy but also when we're in crisis. Let us keep our expectations and our vision high. Whatever we focus on is what we are moving toward. By directing our minds we direct our lives. It is our Creator's wish to give us life in abundance. My monthly editorials in *Essence* and the essays in this book are dedicated to helping us remember that truth.

Each of you, descendent of some passed-
On traveler, has been paid for.
—Maya Angelou
"On the Pulse of Morning"

LIVING
FROM
WITHIN

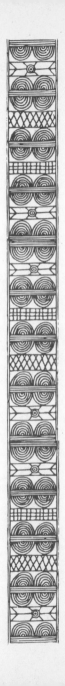

There are glorious times in our lives when we experience the peace we are seeking—when we surrender our burdens to God, put our faith in God's love and feel the freedom of that sweet communion. I know that you, too, have felt the comfort of the Presence—the security we have when focused inward through prayer or meditation. The sense of inner peace we experience listening to a moving sermon or inspirational tape, or reading comforting words of wisdom in a spiritual book. During these times of bliss we often declare, "I've got it, I have the key!" We believe we've finally found our inner peace, that absolute answer we've been searching for. But if your experience is in any way like mine, after a few months, weeks or sometimes just hours you've lost it again, you're back in the fray, feeling overwhelmed by the pressures and demands of your life.

Focusing inward through prayer, meditation or any spiritual communion makes us feel centered and calm. We feel an inner serenity. We are one with God. But why is it so difficult to maintain that awareness, to live with it? My life feels anchored

1 ∎

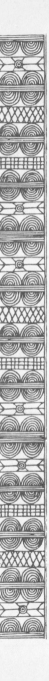

and peaceful when I'm enjoying sunrise meditations, my fragrant candlelit baths and spiritual readings and tapes. But little by little the rituals that sustain me are pushed aside as more and more of my time and attention are demanded by the world.

Although "getting it" can happen in a flash, *keeping* the awareness of God's presence within and the peace of mind this truth gives us is never easy. Unfortunately, as the world calls us, we abandon the important rituals that nourish us, that keep us healthy and sane. The regular visits to the gym go. We have no time to spare for daily meditation, no time to mend the spirit. No time for fun, no time to play. We're overextended. We're committed to everyone—everyone except ourselves. So we feel evil and tired. We're cranky and fretful—we've given all our stuff away.

Being the guardian of our inner life must become our highest priority. We must never allow people, institutions or social tradition to speak to us so loudly that we cannot hear ourselves. When you don't take quiet time, time to listen inwardly, you look outside yourself for salvation and definition. By ignoring your own spiritual bidding, you dishonor yourself and risk becoming a pain-filled impostor as you give way to the pressures in your environment. You may betray yourself and settle for a relationship without intimacy or mutual support—the very things you need most—because you fear being alone and desperately want to be part of a couple. Or you may find yourself anchored to a bustling city when your spirit requires the respite of birds and trees. Or working for a company half your life, unappreciated and undercompensated, when all along your spirit has been whispering, *Start a business of your own*.

When we don't nourish Spirit in us, we become estranged from ourselves and may try to satisfy our natural hunger for communion in harmful ways. There are invitations all around us to use food and drink and other life-threatening addictions to pleasure ourselves. We can't benefit from our inner wisdom if we don't take time to listen inwardly. The wise voice at the center of our being, where Spirit lives, is never silent. Thank God.

Life is first an inner experience. All the peace and security we are seeking is within us. Love, wisdom, strength and beauty are the primary attributes of Spirit, the unchanging and fundamental core of our being. Love, wisdom, strength and beauty are the very substance of who we are. Just as water cannot be separated from a wave, we cannot be separated from our essence, our divinity. We are never without God. But without regular spiritual communion, we forget about our divine nature, we lose the awareness of our spiritual power and ours becomes a halting, feeble existence because we are living without the benefit of our greatest strength.

If we sincerely want harmony, peace and joy in our lives, we can have them, but we must be willing to do the work. We must make maintaining an awareness of our spiritual nature first in our lives. Our inner world is the architect of our external world. We don't lose faith in the goodness of life because we are angry and depressed. Rather, we become angry and depressed because we lose faith in the goodness of life. We aren't happy because we are healthy, we're healthy because we are happy. With our minds we are creating our days; by our choices we are building either the harmony or the pain we experience.

The life you are living reflects the life you have already established inside. As we acquire and assimilate spiritual knowledge, we liberate ourselves. The imaginary boundary between our inner and outer lives that is drawn as we leave childhood and begin looking outside ourselves for definition is dissolved. Immediate and profound changes occur in every area of our lives as we make learning and applying spiritual insights first in importance. We begin to see that the inner and the outer are

3 ■

the same. We realize that continuous communion with God is the only way to remain conscious of our spiritual nature in the face of our constant daily pressures.

When we are conscious of our divinity, we catch the light, we see the truth. We have the wisdom, courage and stamina to endure, to overcome and succeed. As we develop our latent spiritual power, we become the masters of our own lives, and we are able to create lifelines for our people, for our sisters and brothers who are drowning. When we are living from within, we recognize the potential for spiritual growth in each moment.

Living in the spirit isn't complicated. But it does require continual commitment and devotion. Everything necessary to your wholeness is within you. You don't *need* to go to a house of prayer or a mountaintop retreat to commune with God. You don't have to move a muscle. Wherever you are is where God is. You can't always physically remove yourself from the madness of the world for prayer and meditation. But you can always draw upon your inner wisdom—anytime, anyplace. *You can listen inwardly even in a crowded room. Even in the middle of an argument you can heed your higher self and rise above the ego's need to be right and make the other person wrong. During any challenge or conflict you can decide to give way to love.* You can always smile toward your center, where truth and wisdom await you, and say to the Holy Spirit "I surrender."

Living from within is an exercise in self-awareness. It requires consistency in exploring the dynamics of your life—being constantly aware of your feelings, attitudes, habits and motives. As you watch yourself faithfully, you become more aware of what triggers your happy and conflicting emotions, your positive and negative impulses. You become alert to the things that are good for your body and to those that cause it harm. You develop an awareness of the people and things that provoke frustration and anger in you, and those that motivate and inspire you to feel loving and calm.

Self-awareness puts you in control of yourself so that you no longer simply react to life, but instead think critically about what's best for you and consciously decide how you want to be. When we are focused inward and making conscious decisions based on what makes us feel whole, we grow stronger in mind, body and spirit.

The search for yourself is your life's purpose. To know yourself is to know the power of God within you. We are here to discover our truth and to make our unique contribution to life. The universe is supporting us, and Spirit wants us to give something back to help and heal others, but first the healing must begin within us. We must learn to trust the Mystic within. We must learn to recognize and respect God within ourselves.

You and I know these truths, we know the Way. Our challenge is to close the book, to leave the religious service, to turn off the tape— and practice *living* the message. The more we practice living from within— listening and talking to God throughout each day—the more conscious we become of God's indwelling presence, the more receptive our minds and hearts become to the wisdom of Spirit. Then we have deeper insight, and a greater understanding of life. Then our duties, cares and worries become our opportunities for growth, and our burdens are made lighter.

THE POWER OF LOVE

How would you live if you felt you could trust life fully? If you believed you were totally protected and secure, that forevermore your life would be filled with love and prosperity? Think of how your fears would dissolve, of how totally accepting of yourself and others you would be—it wouldn't matter if they met your expectations or not. Think of how you would venture forth *knowing* you would succeed. Think of how your heart would open, of how free you would feel. How free you would be to love. All of this is the treasure that life offers us. We just lack the consciousness to experience it.

We *are* love. We are created in the image and likeness of the Loving Spirit that created us. Each of us is a perfect and powerful child of God, a holy light. But because we've forgotten this truth, we feel separate from God and we experience the pain and confusion of feeling vulnerable. We mistakenly believe we are incomplete. And so our energy is focused on "fixing" and trying to change ourselves and others in unimportant and unrealistic ways. It's this feeling of inadequacy that undermines our self-esteem and makes us hypercritical. Then life becomes

a frustration rather than a fulfilling experience. The absence of loving attitudes and practices is at the root of all our troubles.

We don't have to settle for the anxiety and turmoil that have become the collective consciousness of humanity. Because love is our source and our substance, and because expressing love is the very purpose of our existence, we can return to loving at any moment. Our capacity to love is never lost. We grew up thinking that love is capricious, that when we "misbehave" we are unworthy of love. But God is benevolent. We don't have to earn love, search or struggle to find it. We only need the faith to accept that it flows through us from an inexhaustible source.

The kingdom of love is within you, and that is where you must seek it. It is in the stillness of your own heart. Love is everywhere around you—in everything that God created. You only need to pause for a moment to recognize the Holy Presence—as the night sky, as each blade of grass, as your own heartbeat.

Active love does mighty works. Love can heal us, our relationships and the chaos in our world. Learning to be more loving is the most valuable thing we could ever do. Love casts out fear; it helps us feel happy and whole. In order to live peacefully and harmoniously, our life's work must include learning to love everyone unconditionally, starting with ourselves.

Granted, it is difficult to love those who do unkind things. But the more unlovable a person appears, the more in need of love he is. I had a sisterfriend who absolutely crushed my heart. Throughout a decade of intimate sharing I had grown to love her and trust revealing my deepest feelings to her. She knew how depressed and confused I was when my first marriage was unraveling, and she was there for me. When I was pregnant, lonely and miserable, she would even include me on her dates. When a new relationship suddenly became violent, she was the first person I turned to.

It shocked and hurt me to learn that throughout the years while she was telling me all of her friends' business, she was also telling them mine. This sister, who I felt betrayed me, was greatly unhappy with her own life. She was also one of my greatest teachers. She taught me that those who don't love themselves can't love me, and that people will treat me just as they treat others; she taught me not to invite gossip. She taught me that as I forgive those who hurt me, I, too, am forgiven for the hurts I cause. She challenged me to remember that we all mess up at times, that not one of us is always loving and wise. I still love this sister very much, but now I send her loving, healing thoughts from a distance. Not everyone is healthy enough to have a front-row seat in our lives.

The hurts and disappointments we experience can harden our hearts and make us fearful and distrustful. We may shut the door to our hearts in an effort to protect ourselves from pain. But love cannot flow from a closed heart: It needs an open channel. To give and receive love you have to make contact with life, take risks, know that there will be bitter and sweet experiences. Even your most meaningful relationships will at times challenge you to keep your heart open.

We can't experience the love we crave when we are angry or holding grudges. Bitterness blocks love's flow. And it eats away at the host. A thought that helps me not to be resentful of anyone who hurts or disrespects me is that people can only be who they are. Expecting them to be who we want them to be, or to operate beyond their level of understanding and development, is an exercise in frustration for us and is unfair to them. We'd best accept folks as they are, or let them *grow* on without us.

When you are loving, you are living righteously, so despite the possibility of hurtful experiences, you can never lose. Even when others don't return your goodness, you win, because when you're loving, you're in harmony with life: You feel at one

with the most powerful force in the universe, and all the blessings that flow from love are rushing toward you. As Jesus counseled, "Cast your bread [love] on the water, and it shall return to you." Love is the lifespring of our existence. The more love you give, the happier you feel and the more love you will have within you to give.

With your heart and soul you must strive to be loving in all your ways. *Try to consciously express love whenever you touch someone, through your eyes, smile, thoughts and words, and through your actions.* Love is in urgent need of expressing itself in our world. Love needs you as a channel. You were created for this purpose.

You can enter love's kingdom and experience inexpressible joy just by choosing to turn the key that is your mind. Find a peaceful and relaxing space. Move your attention within. Close your eyes. Slow your breathing. Love is always beckoning you to come back to yourself, to your reality. Feel the love within you flowing from your heart throughout your body. Feel love supporting you, surrounding you. Rest here for a moment, in the heart of God. Remind yourself that you needn't ever fear failure, illness or any misfortune—that love is the unchanging foundation of life and you are always in love's embrace.

Now hold yourself in your own arms—tenderly, just as you would hold a child you love dearly. Hug yourself. Gently rock yourself. Whisper "I love you" to your heart. This is your healing time. Lay your burdens down. Smile from your heart and feel any hurt, anger or fear dissolving. Imagine love and light warming any part of your body that is experiencing illness. Feel love and light encircling you. Widen the circle to include your family and friends and anyone who needs love and light. Offer a prayer for our people, for all of the people in the world. Stay quiet with yourself for a few minutes and experience the bliss of feeling centered in love. Promise yourself to return here often. Demonstrating love for yourself is the cornerstone of your happiness and the way to begin to help our people and heal the world.

Love is life-generating. If you attempt to practice loving, even for a few minutes, your life will begin to change. By thinking and acting as if you are grounded in love, you open a channel for the Holy Spirit to express itself through you.

Under the influence of love, everything in your life gets better. Clouds begin to dissipate and your sense of inner freedom expands. You realize that you are free to love, free to be, free to create the good life you envision. And so your life becomes the joyful journey that God promises.

Renew
YOUR
FAITH

How do you feel about life? Are you looking to the future with hope and enthusiasm because you believe good things will happen, or do you feel fearful and worried because you believe hard times lie ahead? In either case, your positive or negative faith is creating your future. Your perspective on life determines how you see yourself, how you live each day and how you relate to the world.

Faith is potent stuff: It's a generator. What we believe is the starting point of what we experience. I remember how that truth was brought home to me one evening. After a particularly trying day at work, I was dashing about the city running errands. Tired and tense, I felt put-upon, even hostile. I remember thinking *If anybody dares to mess with me tonight* . . . Well, within minutes I was embroiled in a senseless argument with a complete stranger. Not his fault—mine. My negative faith had created the space for a negative experience.

We can make our lives a dance or a dirge; our attitude makes the difference. It's one of nature's laws: What you give to life and what you expect from it are what you will get—in exactly

the same measure. Either you consciously walk in the light of faith and love, or you wander in the darkness of doubt and fear and your life becomes a continuous struggle.

What I cherish most about our existence is that no matter how bad circumstances may appear, it is always possible to make them better. At any time we choose, we can begin getting our lives back on track, feeling joyous once again—if we are willing to give up negative thoughts and habits and replace them with positive ones. The only time positive faith fails us is when we fail to use it.

Having faith doesn't mean sitting back and waiting for miracles. *Life* is the miracle. *You* are the miracle. You are made in the image and likeness of God in that you, too, have the power to create great things. But first you must believe in your innate power. Then you must move your feet. You must set high goals and work toward them consistently. God doesn't do the work for you, but through you.

Renew your faith. Know that life always has something very special in store for you and that all of your experiences— including the painful and shameful ones—have value when you begin using them as tools for growth.

Affirm your individual beauty, your intelligence and our legacy as a people—our inner strength and tenacity in overcoming adversity. Yes, we live in a racist and sexist society, which makes it difficult to keep our faith strong. Oppressed people are always engaged in a draining struggle. But if we are to win our fight for equity, we must first envision our power and our victory. Little in the larger society reminds us of how capable we are, so we must continuously affirm ourselves and one another.

Negative thoughts and actions block love, wisdom, clarity and prosperity—the gifts that flow from God. So how do you turn away from negativity? By becoming a watchperson at your mind's door. *Close the door on each negative imagining and consciously replace it with a positive one that you would like to take root in your life. Challenge yourself each moment to act only on the positive principals, the ones that you know are of God.*

Once you begin to practice living with positive faith, you become aware of the great opportunities available to you each day. You see that with conscious effort and hard work you can have a fulfilling life, you can do your part to secure our children. You aren't weighed down by problems. You are focused on finding solutions. You feel strong. You have zest and drive, and the veil of negativity is lifted.

Once the cycle of negativity is broken, your faith in yourself and the goodness of life is restored. You realize that you have the capacity to meet all your needs. So you begin planning and acting in accordance with that faith and find that you *do* have

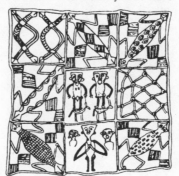

enough patience, enough creativity, energy, money and all that is needed to live fully. Your faith in the providence and generosity of life is reinforced. And the more you believe in the natural abundance of life, the more of it you experience, the more passionately you work to make life better for others.

15 ▪

LIVING YOUR FAITH

We learn most about the unlimited breadth and depth of God's love for us when our faith is tested. Often it's when we are at the point of despair, when we have exhausted all of our limited human solutions, that we finally surrender to God and trust the Holy Spirit to have its way in us.

It has been so with me. During times of crisis my faith has been so shaken that I feared my life would never get better. But it's also been in my darkest hours—when my reasoning mind fails to see the larger spiritual cycles at work—that I've grown in awareness of God's unfailing love and infinite power. The seeds of faith are always alive in us, but sometimes it takes a crisis to provoke them to grow.

It's true that a worried mind saps energy, feeds the blues and fuels a negative cycle. But sometimes a case of the blues is one of the ways God beckons us. My greatest insights have been shaped by my greatest challenges. The same is probably true for you. Life is very much like a schoolroom: It gives us the lessons and tests we need to develop and grow. Every crisis in our lives is a call toward the Holy One. If, early on, we can

recognize the opportunity for growth inherent in each obstacle in our path, we will reduce the amount of energy expended and pain endured in repeating the same lessons.

We all want to avoid pain and suffering as much as possible, but they are intrinsic to life. Although we cannot totally avoid emotional pain, we can get a jump on handling it at the first symptom. Just as you might treat yourself with vitamin C to stave off a cold, treating yourself with a dose of active faith—making a conscious effort to stand firm and to put your faith in God—will stave off fear and lead you toward a new beginning.

Once a crisis is history, you can easily look back on it and see how the experience expanded your awareness and helped you to grow. But it is while you are at a critical juncture that you must resist giving your power to panic, anger or fear. This is when you must use your power to tame your mind and have faith in the truth: Spirit is always at the center of your being; therefore, everything in your life, regardless of appearances, is in Divine Order. *During any crisis, pause before you act and focus your energy inward to your highest state of consciousness, where infinite knowledge, wisdom and strength abide.*

Each time we face and grow through a painful situation, we are made stronger, wiser, whole again. Intellectual insecurity coaxed me to return to school. Financial and emotional struggles as a single mother compelled me to become more focused, more disciplined, to *get* up when I wanted to *give* up.

Our biggest problems in life come not so much from the difficulties we confront but from how we perceive and respond to them. I've stayed depressed for weeks before remembering I had a choice: I could continue to dwell on the problem and the many ways in which it could ruin my life, or I could take charge of my thoughts, uplift my faith and move my feet in a positive direction. If we act with the confidence of faith when facing life's daily difficulties and frustrations, each day we will bring our faith forward, increasing and strengthening it. Then we will have the inner assurance and the emotional strength to surmount the big stuff. As you practice awareness of the Presence within you as a conscious moment-to-moment mental exercise, living your faith becomes a life habit.

The habit of faith is as simple as the habit of facing the light instead of the dark when you want to see. Toward the light is the truth: Everything you need to live fully will always be provided.

N*EW* *BEGINNINGS*

This is the big one:

You've procrastinated. Your body is in bad shape, your health is waning. Debts are overwhelming you. You see no way out of the present quagmire, so you've given up planning your future.

Or. . .

You've made a mistake. A huge error in judgment. One so grave and costly you believe it will never be forgotten, never be forgiven. You will never forgive yourself.

Or. . .

You believe your life is shattered forever because of an unwelcome life change: A job is lost, a partner is gone. Someone, something that has long been a part of your identity, that gave your life meaning, is stripped away. You feel your value and worth threatened.

Whatever it is, something is causing you great emotional pain. You feel so bad you doubt you'll ever be happy again. It happens to us all: An incident takes place, a mishap occurs, a series of wrong choices catches up with us. As long as we are

alive, no matter how old or how young we are, we'll face
unforeseen, life-altering trials.

An incident occurred when I was a youngster that lay heavily
on my heart and that I thought would ruin my life forever. A boy
named Melvin had moved from St. Thomas into the Harlem
tenement where my family and I lived. I was only 11 years old,
but Melvin made my heart quicken. Truth be told, I was a
precocious child who was always testing the limits and might
have taken the lead in orchestrating our first caress.

One cold rainy evening in November, Melvin and I agreed to
meet again just before the dinner hour on the top flight of the
back stairwell. He arrived before I did and was waiting with a
big sweet smile as I ascended the steps. Suddenly we heard
footsteps and the jangle of a dog's chain leash getting closer.
Someone was coming up the back stairway and turned the
corner as we bolted onto the roof. In a flash Melvin was gone.
He jumped across the narrow alley onto the rooftop of the
building next door and disappeared into the night. I thank God
I didn't panic and attempt that leap myself, because I surely
would have fallen to my death. So there I was, trapped, face-to-
face with our neighbor Mr. Bailey, who was walking his dog on
the roof that evening. When he asked me what I was doing up
there with Melvin, I mumbled, stumbled, told a quick lie and
ran past him down several flights to my second-floor apartment. My heart was beating hard and fast, but not so wildly as
it did later that evening when Mr. Bailey appeared at my door
to tell my mother about his discovery of me and Melvin
together.

It was a living nightmare. Even now my heart races at the
memory. Had you known my strict, puritanical and overly pro-
tective West Indian father—who was already 48 when I was
born—you would fully understand why. That evening I begged
my mother not to tell him, to spare my life. But after Daddy
closed his store and came upstairs, Mommy broke the news.

I don't remember my father saying a single word to me that night—or many words in subsequent years—but the anger in his eyes spoke volumes, and he gave me the whipping of my life. The wounds that were left weren't physical, they were emotional. I felt ashamed. Alienated. As though an icy wall had been raised with me on one side, my parents and my older brother on the other.

Within weeks we moved out of the inner city into the home my parents had purchased earlier that fall. I was so relieved. I could create a new life. I wouldn't have to avoid the many neighbors who I was sure had heard about the roof incident. In my new Queens neighborhood (unlike crowded Spanish Harlem) there were wide-open spaces, kids on bikes, sewing classes, summer barbecues, block parties—and people who didn't know about my past. But not until I graduated from high school and left home to build a life of my own did I feel any familial warmth. Only then did the icy wall begin to thaw, and the separation begin to heal.

We all know what it's like to carry emotional burdens. In our lifetime we'll struggle with shame, loss, depression, guilt— the gamut of human emotions that can vanquish us if we allow them to. However, it is this very ability to feel, to experience the full range of passions, that makes us human, that connects us with life and with one another.

We are conditioned early on to deny powerful, painful emotions. For many years I refused even to think about that traumatic childhood experience. I buried it deep within myself when I moved from the old tenement on 116th Street. I made a clear and conscious decision never to think about it or mention it to anyone. But stifling or denying painful feelings doesn't make them go away. Eventually those little demons will jump you from behind.

I spent years running away from myself. I ran to material things, I ran to religion, I ran to relationships. I looked for love

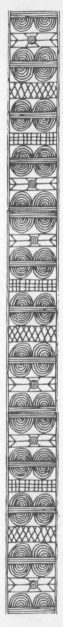

and acceptance in the wrong places. When I could run no longer because I was weary and depressed, I began, finally, the difficult task of facing myself. I stopped running away from those aspects of my past that frightened or shamed me, and I tried to understand how they were shaping my life.

It took me years to work through the shame of the sensual exploring I did as a little girl. After much soul-searching, I began to put the incident on the roof and my parents' reaction to it into perspective. The more closely I examined it, the more clearly I could see the lessons in it: My parents weren't always right, but they were the perfect parents for the path I'm on. Both the pain and the pleasures we shared brought me to this place in my life. Their reaction to my exploration was also an early lesson in sexism. Had my brother Larry been caught kissing a girl on the stairs, I know that my parents' reaction would not have been harsh, but the girl's parents would probably have reacted as mine did. That life experience has been of great value to me as a mother. Although I haven't always been successful, I've tried to be open with Shana-Nequai and to be understanding and compassionate while correcting and protecting her.

We unburden ourselves by examining our emotional baggage and holding it up to the light. Carrying forward anything that makes us pity ourselves, feel bad about how we've acted or feel guilty about what we've not attended to will lead us to treat ourselves unkindly. Anything that is weighing you down is made lighter if you take it to God. Then you're not running away from yourself, but summoning the courage to *be* with yourself, in stillness, in silence, where you will perceive the good that was created from the experience.

My friend Andriette Earl-Bozeman says that meditation helps her maintain balance in her life: ''Through the simple process of being silent, focusing, listening, affirming myself and visualizing the positive things I want in my life, I am filling the huge hole created by years of pain and self-neglect." Andriette testifies that meditation has given her the "constitution to do with love this dance called life."

Every experience has good fallout. What I felt was a shameful experience that put a damper on my sexuality actually prevented me from becoming pregnant as a teenager. The powerful sexual longings I felt as a child, coupled with my rebellious and adventurous nature, would surely have led me to have sex early. Throughout my teens, because I really believed my father would have killed me had I gotten pregnant, there was no way I allowed any boyfriend to enter me. So in drive-in theaters and secluded spots surrounding Baisley Park, I discovered the universe of pleasure between sexual abstinence and consummation—information I would pass on to my daughter. In retrospect, my parents' sternness developed in me the discipline and inner will that I need to survive and thrive today.

You can relieve any pressure and renew your life by trusting in God. God's kingdom isn't in the heavens or in the hereafter. God is wherever you are. The kingdom is right here, right now, closer than your next breath. *Any healing that you need can take place within you, in the stillness of your being. No special prayers or chants or mantras are needed here. All you must do is get quiet and ask the Holy Spirit to give you understanding and peace.*

We bring about new beginnings by deciding to bring about endings. To renew your life you must be willing to change, to make an effort to leave behind the things that compromise your wholeness. The universe rushes to support you whenever you attempt to take a step forward. Any time you seek to be in harmony with life, to make yourself feel more whole, all the blessings that flow from God stream toward you, to bolster you and encourage you, because all life is biased on the side of supporting itself.

Our understanding of our humanness is underdeveloped and distorted, causing inner tension and pressure when our

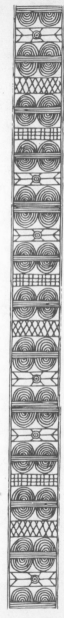

25 ■

lives don't fit society's mold. You must value *all* of your history, including the painful parts. The more you deny your pain, the more you are bound to it. The more you accept it, the more you can use it to understand yourself and help others.

All your experiences are valid and important. Everything in your past happened for a reason. Each of your experiences is a step that is leading you to a right and better place.

POSSIBILITIES

"In the beginning was the Word." So goes the poetic and profound statement in the Bible. In half a dozen words it sums up the whole of creation. Look around you. Nothing, from the wheel to the jet plane, was ever crafted by human beings that did not first find existence in a word, a thought, a concept, an intangible seed of energy: Spirit.

There is intelligence in the energy that surrounds us. Preachers have preached this, philosophers have proclaimed it. It's a simple truth in the Bible: "Thou shalt decree a thing and it shall be established unto thee and the light shall shine upon thy way" (Job 22:28). The creative power of our thoughts, words and actions gives form to the energy in the universe. Life is energy. Breath is energy. Thought is energy. An unlimited supply of energy is all around us and is ours to shape as we will. Our every idea, word and action reverberate into the universe, creating a pathway through which that same vibration returns to us, made manifest as an experience. Whatever you radiate, you attract. Whatever you express, you create a channel for

27 ■

receiving. It is a spiritual law, as immutable as the law of action and reaction in physics.

Our divinity gives us dominion. This is God's promise. We know this, but we don't trust it. We possess the creative energy to "re-form" our lives, to reshape the world. Although we have the power to fulfill our divine plan, few of us do. Most people settle for small lives. We *sense* our divinity and the great possibilities that life offers us, but we limit ourselves because of fear and lack of faith.

We fear change and resist it because it threatens the order—or disorder—in our lives. Change always means leaving something or someone behind, and breaking with the past forces us to question deeply and do the work of recreating our lives.

We limit ourselves because change may well mean dealing with the disapproval of the very people we rely on for support. The career move you want to make means going back to school, but your partner puts up a fuss because you won't be home at 6:30 each evening. You want to be an artist, but your parents tell you that you'll starve, that they didn't send you to school to learn how to draw. Sometimes we dishonor what fulfills us most just to avoid conflict. Doubts and insecurities undermine our belief in ourselves and make us feel afraid to go against the tide or break with the familiar past. But we must weed out the old—whether it's clutter that's crowding our home or ideas or habits that are not in harmony with our center—to make room for the new. Life is about transformation.

We are not powerless spectators of life. We are cocreators with God, and all around us are the gifts, the raw material that we can use to shape our world. The very matter we are made of is the fulfillment of a promise made to us by God's words in the beginning: "Let there be light!" Each of us is an expression of that light—living energy, life. Dare to believe that you can live as fully and as prosperously as you can imagine. You are not just a part of the Great Cosmic Force, you *are* the Force. Your mind is the connecting link between the formed and the unformed world.

You need only apply the alchemy of faith and action to your positive ideas. Speak the word, perform the tasks, and you lay the foundation for success through the same creative channel that first created the universe. Your thoughts are the seeds that grow the conditions in your life. Whatever you wish to achieve awaits your calling it forth—perfect health, a beautiful home, a supportive relationship, a new and better life. Continue to name it and work at achieving it.

We create the things we don't want in our lives the very same way—by holding negative images, ideas and thoughts in the mind and then affirming them verbally. "I can't" is the building block of our biggest defeats, our largest failures. Your thoughts and words have the creative power to support your doubts and to undo your best efforts. The universe will agree with whatever you feel and speak and plan in earnest. If you feel you are unable to reach lofty goals, you will have neither the desire nor the energy to attain them. If you don't feel you deserve to be prosperous, you will make no place for prosperity in your life. If you are distrustful of people, you will attract those who aren't worthy of your trust. The conditions of your life mirror the energy you send forth into the universe. By harboring anger and pain, you attract the people and the circumstances that keep your anger and pain alive. But if you place your faith in the love and security that a perfectly reliable and organized universe ensures, you will attract those people and experiences that support your feelings of love and security. What you think, say and plan for is what you will realize. Like gravity, the law of attraction is an unchanging law.

We have to declare ownership of our lives. With conviction and with a force equal to the law of gravity behind it, declare "I am in charge of me,

of my thoughts and actions, and I have the power to live my heart's desires."
We are held back only by our limited knowledge of ourselves and limited belief in our capabilities. Rather than curse what you feel is missing in your life, bless the many riches you take for granted—the ability to think, speak and create. You can have it all—all that you desire—if you lay the foundation.

You are created in the image and likeness of God. You have Godpower. As much as the stars, the trees and the rivers, you are both the word and voice of God. The Mind, the Word— these powers that gave birth to the universe are all yours. Claim them and use them to create the life you want.

Declare that you are now free of self-doubt and fear, unfettered by limitations. Put your trust in God and live each day committed to positive thoughts and actions. Then you are building your spiritual factory, harnessing the intelligent energy surrounding you, shaping it your way. The power is yours. It is within you, waiting to be radiated outward, into the universe, to do your bidding.

LIFE
IS A
JOURNEY

Life is a journey, not a destination. Those were the provocative words on a poster hanging on the wall in my friends' home in Jamaica years ago. I was in my early twenties, newly married, immature. The many times when it seemed that my life was falling apart, if I could find the money I would escape to the island paradise and the comfort of Pat and Ken Ramsay's love. *Life is a journey, not a destination*—I remember staring at the words, whispering them, trying to fathom their meaning as I rocked in the hammock that hung near the intriguing poster.

Life is a journey, not a destination. All these years later I'm beginning to grasp the meaning. Life is a process, a learning experience. We don't discover all of life's answers at once, but over time, through many and varied—and necessary—experiences. We will have hundreds of arrivals. And still we will not have reached life's destination. As long as we are alive, we are in the process of becoming.

The purpose of our journey is to learn to live in harmony with the reciprocal laws of life: to love our neighbor as ourself

and to trust that whatever we give to life comes back multiplied. It is to understand that we can never withdraw from life what we have not invested in it. Love and reciprocity, these are the laws of creation that we are here to discover and live by. Wherever we are on our life's journey, we are always moving toward this realization.

Each of us comes to the awareness of the truth in her or his own way. Some of our lessons are easily learned; others are incredibly difficult. But we are all expanding our knowledge of ourselves and the meaning of life all the time. There are lessons in wealth, lessons in poverty, in victory, defeat and physical challenge. While one of us is learning lessons by raising a child, another is learning by losing a child. Near the end of his life, tennis great and humanitarian Arthur Ashe said that people would invariably ask him if he was angry, if he felt cheated because he was dying of AIDS and if he ever asked "Why me?" Arthur said that he didn't feel angry or cheated, that if he asked "Why me?" about contracting AIDS and his imminent death, he would have to ask "Why me?" about all the good fortune and many blessings that were also a part of his extraordinary life.

The religious scholar Pierre Teilhard de Chardin taught, "To be spiritualized is to be de-materialized." Matter is not the source of life, of consciousness. *Life is more subtle, and more substantial, than it appears. All the daily affairs that engross you—your goals, your relationships, the blessings that delight you, the challenges that make you struggle—are the Creator's way of engaging you, focusing your attention so that you keep moving onward, keep correcting your course and putting your faith in the laws of love and reciprocity.*

In a sense life is very impersonal. Though we make judgments about whether our experiences are good or bad, we should not take the individual experiences personally. They are our schooling, the episodes with which life seasons us. This is easy to say but difficult to accept when we feel we're confronting disaster: A hurricane destroys our home, our town, and renders us and thousands more homeless; a person we love dearly seems lost to drugs; tests show that we have developed a debilitating illness. It is difficult to recognize the opportunity for growth while experiencing loss and pain, but the fact is that nature is always constructing and reconstructing itself. The old is constantly surrendering to the new. Everything we experience on life's road is to move us toward greater love and charity, to make us draw closer to ourselves, closer to one another, closer to God.

We are daughters and sons of God. We, too, are divine. Each and every experience is an encouragement to have faith in our divinity, to strive to achieve higher consciousness, which is the purpose of our journey. Jesus' life should confirm for us that we are human and divine. Jesus, too, had human doubts and fears, but he achieved Christhood because he kept renewing his faith in God, in the laws of love and reciprocity. And throughout his adult life, he tested and applied them. The Bible tells us that with five loaves and two fishes he fed the multitudes. That through his faith the lame walked, the blind were made to see. All because he believed in his divinity and used his divine power to inspire others to believe in their wholeness as well. Remember the promise: These things and even greater works you can do if, like Jesus, you have faith in your divine nature and strive to express love in your every word, deed and action. Jesus' life is an example of what each of us is destined to become.

Life is a journey, a journey in self-discovery, in discovering our enormous individual power. We have the power to build. We can rebuild a home, a city, a nation. Like our brother Jesus, each living soul has dominion, each one of us has the power to heal. We can heal ourselves, one another and our world. We are responsible for how we use our power at every step of our journey.

As we accept the good things life offers, we must also be prepared to meet its challenges. What choice do we really have, since challenges are unavoidable? No person journeys through life without facing contradiction and duality. Each of us will know joy and pain, laughter and tears, hope and despair, sometimes in overlapping measure. There are sure to be successes, failures, accolades, insults—and change, change, change.

There is so much to master in the journey of a lifetime: lessons of patience, humility, generosity, forgiveness and more. Buddhists put their faith in Karma, the law of cause and effect—that what goes around, comes around. They believe that the soul journeys through many lifetimes and we are born into each life with both the blessings we have earned and the lessons we have not yet learned in previous lifecycles.

Everything we experience along our journey—however pleasant or difficult it may be—is a lesson in living. If we approach life with this basic understanding and with the clarity and vision gained through the faith that we are always moving forward, we will see how the valleys and the rough places lead us to higher ground, to the mountaintop experiences.

We journey for a purpose: to become compassionate and wise, to become healers and teachers. To learn to trust stepping away from the crowd and committing ourselves to love. We were born to be reborn. Sometimes our lessons come daily, sometimes by the hour, but always our birth is an unending act. Life is a journey. It's a journey toward our truest self. It's a journey toward the light.

PERSONAL NOTES ON SELF-LOVE

Self-love. It's the starting point for giving love to others. It opens the door to abundant living. Without it we limp through life, become part of the walking wounded, the living dead. Self-love. Our cornerstone. We can't grow or glow without it. It determines how solid and fulfilling our lives are. It's the foundation on which we build all the rest.

Intellectually, we know the power and the importance of loving ourselves. But often we have difficulty practicing self-caring. Sometimes we meet a wall of cultural conditioning that says it's selfish to focus on or pamper ourselves. But this is confusing self-love with hedonism—exclusive self-involvement that has no resemblance to the practice of love. When we don't satisfy our own mental, physical and spiritual need for love, depression and illness overtake us. Spirit forces us to retreat, and perhaps it's then that we begin listening to ourselves, loving and honoring our needs, so that our healing can begin.

Some years ago, just after I'd become editor-in-chief of *Essence*, a stunning depression took hold of me. I couldn't figure out why I was feeling so miserable. It should have been a great

time in my life. Although many people didn't believe I had the
intelligence or skill to run the magazine—and said as much to
our publisher, Ed Lewis—Ed believed in me and promoted me
to the top spot from the fashion and beauty editor's position.
Now, finally, I was making enough money for me and my
daughter, Shana-Nequai, to live without having to count every
single dime—I could pay my gas bill *and* my phone bill each
month. It was summer and Shana was staying with my mother
and my sister, Lillian, in Queens. My pumpkin could ride her
bike, jump rope and play outside with her friends, and I didn't
have to do the daily dash home by six o'clock to fix dinner,
check homework, braid hair and the rest.

Our editorial team had breathed new life into the magazine,
and our readership was growing. I was in love with a wonderful
and brilliant brother who was loving me back. So what could
have been so wrong in my life? Why couldn't I stop crying? Why
was I feeling so disconnected, so unhappy? One evening after
work, I somehow instinctively knew that what I needed only I
could give to myself. So that night, for the first time, rather than
reaching out to a sisterfriend or to my man to help me feel
better, I decided to spend the evening alone.

I went home and put on Aretha's music. I drew a warm bath,
added my fragrant oils and lit my candles. I immersed myself
in the calm of the water with no plan other than to relax and,
I hoped, to soothe and comfort myself. Lying low and breathing
easy I heard myself whisper, "Hello, beautiful!" I called my own
self "Sweetie Pie." It sounded so strange. But it felt so good.
It lifted my spirits, made me smile. Suddenly I felt my arms
wrapping around my own body. I began holding myself in my
own embrace, kissing my shoulders, my arms, my knees—
every part of my body I could reach. It wasn't a sexual experience but a deeply sensuous and healing one. It was a laying on
of hands. Me celebrating myself.

For so long I had been living outside of myself, trying to be a good mother, a good daughter, a good editor, a good lover, a good friend. All my energy had been focused outside of me, on others, on trying to be right for them. That evening I saw clearly what was happening to me. Although I had some of the trappings of success, I was feeling empty inside. I hadn't been loving myself in active ways, in ways that preserve.

Although we talk a lot about the importance of self-love, very few of us practice it in a real way. As I lay cocooned in the warmth and safety of the water and my own arms, a floodgate of tears was released. I felt relieved, renewed. I knew that to survive I had to hold on to this glorious feeling by regularly carving out time to listen to myself, to affirm and heal myself.

While humility is a virtue, we must also make honoring ourselves part of our private time. *Congratulate yourself for getting through each day, for attending to your many responsibilities. Make honoring yourself an important ritual in your life. No one but you has the time or inclination to tell you regularly how naturally beautiful and capable you are.*

Making a commitment to care for and nurture yourself helps you get out of bed to make that early-morning exercise class. Self-love gives you the discipline to push your belly away from the table when you're satisfied, before you're stuffed full. Self-love will take you back to school for the information or degree you need to move your life forward. It will help you choose wisely—you will refuse the people and things that detract from your well-being. When we are loving ourselves, we are concerned about our future. We are eager to save money for a new home, a business venture or anything that offers greater independence. Self-love moves us to affirm ourselves, to delight in our individual beauty and to be accepting of the physical changes that occur as we mature. Affirming yourself keeps you true to your vision and propels you to find your own best ways to serve humanity.

The feeling of renewal that I experienced that unforgettable

37 ■

evening was a turning point in my life. I learned that caring for ourselves must be our conscious lifetime *recommitment*, that we don't need anyone's permission to be good to ourselves. In order to maintain balance in our lives and achieve our goals while supporting others, we must make self-nurturance and renewal a regular and important part of our lives. In order to think critically, move wisely and give love to others, we must begin with a full cup, a cup that only we ourselves can fill.

THE
HIGHEST
POWER

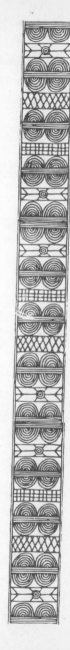

There is a force that supports all existence. It is the energy that governs every aspect of the universe and orders every cell in every living thing. It is unfailing, always at work. It is our source and our substance, an unlimited power that we call by many names: Jehovah, Yahweh, Allah, Divine Intelligence, Spirit, God.

Most of us agree that there is a Highest Power. We testify to that truth. But to experience the inner peace we are seeking, we must do more than speak and sing its name to the heavens. We must keep the awareness that the Power lives within us. It's difficult to sustain trust in the unseen when we're taught to believe only in what is visible. So we put our faith in the material world, when the greatest power is in the nonvisible, spiritual world.

We all want material things, and we work hard to get them. But we surrender the very freedom we are seeking when we believe possessions will make us happy, secure or content. We will always hunger for more when we look to the material world to sustain us. We can see the result of this misplaced faith all

around us: It fuels most of the pain and suffering in the world. Even the wealthiest people don't feel they have enough money. Most want more, and some use any means to get it. They create wars, foul the environment, hook children on drugs, market cancer-causing foods, close factories and ship jobs offshore where even poorer people can be exploited—all to make more money.

When we believe that money gives us our essential power, we let down our moral guard and give up our humanity. We no longer concern ourselves with preserving and enhancing life, so our divinity is stifled and demeaned. When we believe our power is in the material world, we never feel quite strong enough or confident enough or attractive enough to live fully and freely. We always feel that something is lacking, that we should have more. We will violate ourselves trying to boost our self-image so that people will admire us more.

We all want people to like and admire us, but when we *need* their confirmation or adulation, we don't live our lives on our own terms. We are focused outward, intent on surrounding ourselves with the trappings they undoubtedly admire. We were not created to please people. We were created to please God, to recognize the Highest Power in ourselves and make it manifest in our daily lives.

The Highest Power is love and it protects us and all of creation. Love is the very nature of the energy we call God. It is the force that orders this universe and is greater than we can fully comprehend. It choreographs the movements of the more than 200 billion stars, including our sun, hurtling through space—all spinning, spiraling, whirling and revolving in billions of galaxies like the one we live in. Imagine such a power, ordering planets and comets and moons through aeons, in a perfect cosmic dance. Our African ancestors discovered the laws of life thousands of years ago. They understood that the same power that governs the cosmos and protects the lilies of the field sustains us too.

Love yourself as a beautiful and necessary light that was created by God. Remember that the Highest Power is alive within you. It is alive as you. You are human and divine. As is true of the universe, nothing about you is haphazard or accidental. Know that the channels for your existence were put into place in the very beginning. You were created on purpose, with a purpose. You are exactly who and where you need to be, with all the power you need to take your next steps forward. Accept yourself as you are, and make any changes in your life based on your discoveries of what is best for you, what nourishes you and celebrates God through you.

Lift up your faith in yourself and in the miracle that is your being. You never doubt that tomorrow the sun will rise. Have faith that you, too, are an important part of creation. You, too, are protected by love. Don't put your faith in transitory things: They are here today and gone tomorrow. Put your faith in God, the unseen source of all goodness. Make a ritual of spending quiet time, time to focus inward so that you can experience God, the Highest Power, the source of wisdom and strength in you. The Holy Spirit that awaits you at the center of your being.

41 ∎

A
WINNING
ATTITUDE

I came of age feeling confident, capable and strong, as though I could do anything I chose to do. That was how I felt in my late teens, when I started studying acting and winning small parts. I had great self-assurance when as a young woman I completed cosmetology school and started my own cosmetics company. In my early twenties, with only a commercial high-school diploma and without any writing experience, my unwavering confidence led me to present myself at *Essence* for a job. The editor-in-chief at the time, Ida Lewis, believed in me because *I* believed in me, and she offered me the beauty editor's position.

But as my star began to rise at the magazine and I was promoted from beauty editor to fashion and beauty editor to editor-in-chief, my confidence began to waver. It seemed that once I reached the top spot I was invited to present myself everywhere from church pulpits to Capitol Hill and to speak about issues I wasn't well versed in. I could avoid those events easily enough by saying I was unavailable. But when my work began exposing me to more and more high-achievers, my self-

confidence was shaken as I measured myself against the yard-stick of these remarkable people's educational background and achievements.

I've been surrounded by some of the best minds and most accomplished people in the world: sisters and brothers who we would all agree have achieved greatness. They are heads of state and political activists; award-winning writers, editors and scholars; presidents of colleges and universities; great artists; highly talented actors, dancers and designers; the most beautiful models in the world. At times in their company I would lose sight of my own beauty and success. I would forget the enormous sacrifices that my parents made to raise their children and to get us through high school, and my own sacrifices and struggles as a young single mother on the career fast track. While I was greatly inspired by these high-achievers, there were times when I made them models of perfection, compared myself with them and diminished the wonder of my own life.

If maintaining self-confidence became an issue for me in my immediate world of supportive people who look like me, for sisters and brothers in environments where most of the images of power and greatness are White males—and where the structures and systems negate our achievements, intelligence and beauty—maintaining a positive sense of self can be an awesome battle.

When I started recognizing how comparing myself with others was undermining my self-esteem, I began taking periodic inventory of my achievements. While few of us Black folks were born to the manor, we often regard the struggle from where we began our lives to where we are today as "no big thing." For many of us, surviving our neighborhoods means not having gotten caught in the undertow of poverty, drugs and violence. If today we're in school or working, it says we're keeping our sanity in what are often hostile environments—while trying to move ahead, while taking care of family, friends and ourselves and the many tasks those responsibilities require. Given the many pressures in our lives, the fact that we keep getting up and going every day is reason enough to celebrate.

What is your attitude about your life? Do you fully appreciate the distance you've traveled? Do you value your accomplishments? How we view ourselves means everything to us because it determines how we feel inside and how we move through the world.

While we must feel connected to the world around us so that we are able to function and interact in it, we must also remain independent of the superficial ways in which society measures success.

Our judgments of success are too often based on appearances. Through my work I've come to see that many wealthy high-achievers are also miserable people. We envy others' success without considering their struggles or pain. I measure success differently these days. Now I equate it with happiness, personal satisfaction and being of service to others.

If we feel "less than" in anyone's presence, it's because we are making assumptions about that person's life and not seeing our own clearly. And I can tell you from my own experience that when we continually doubt ourselves, we become divorced from ourselves, jealous and fearful.

We must remember that each of us is, as spiritual leader Olga Butterworth says, "a divine original." We are created by God to make a unique contribution to life, one that only we can make. This is as true for you and me, and for the millions who are unknown outside their small circles, as it is for world-renowned champions like Winnie Mandela, Jesse Jackson and Michael Jordan. The more actively we work at trusting and accepting ourselves, the less we'll compare ourselves with people we greatly admire and buy into the myth of our own inadequacy. If we want to feel confident, we have to make the effort to surrender self-negating habits.

We encourage a winning attitude by thinking and speaking about ourselves in loving and self-affirming ways. If you don't love who you are, but only what you wish to become, how will you ever achieve your goals? If you don't acknowledge your value or your winning qualities, how can you use them to achieve?

A negative attitude about where you are in life creates a losing cycle because you constantly criticize yourself, and that leads to self-doubt and feelings of diminished self-worth. We must admit our errors without deprecating ourselves or allowing anyone else to put us down. We should examine our lives critically and honestly, learn from our mistakes and try to keep a "getting up" spirit. Life wears us down if we don't keep ourselves up. I feel great when I'm striving for excellence and competing only with myself. I easily maintain a feeling of surety when I'm around affirming and positive people and when I exercise, rest and do my spiritual work regularly.

When we're not meeting our own needs, we develop a negative attitude toward ourselves and life. This can lead to great unhappiness, all sorts of addictions and eventual mental illness. Through quiet reflection we develop the wisdom and courage to love ourselves as we are and to do the work necessary to create the self and the future we want. With a clear sense of ourselves, we make our own best choices, and by doing so we affirm our dignity and self-worth.

What you love doing is what you've been put here to do. With an attitude of self-acceptance, you won't *first* consider what others think you should be doing; rather, your priority will be what feels right for you. When I spoke about wanting to go to college, people would invariably tell me that I would be wasting time because I was already at the top of my career, well-known and making good money. They'd advise me to read books. What they said made sense, but it wasn't true for me. I didn't want to earn a degree to add a line to my bio or to get a better job. I wanted to go to college to gain information and skills and be more proficient at what I was already doing, so I could stop faking it and feel better about myself. And I knew I'd never buy books about most of the things I eventually learned in college—I knew that I needed the discipline of the classroom.

The closer we get to clearing our heads of other people's beliefs and images of us, the more self-assured and accomplished we will become. We are never too old to write a new chapter. We don't grow old solely because of the aging process, but because we stop dreaming and reaching and trying new adventures. We age when we give up seeking, when we retire from living. Strive to keep a childlike sense of wonder and awe. Thrill to what is new, challenging and exciting. Life is dynamic, it's always moving forward. Are you in the forward flow of life? Are you planning and working toward a happy and fulfilling future?

Renew your attitude about yourself. Take charge of the thoughts and feelings you have about your life. Any obstacles in your path turn to dust once you focus on and believe in your own attributes. You have the power to succeed despite any disabilities—real or imagined. Even if people tell you that you needn't try or that you don't have what it takes to achieve a goal, don't believe the lie. Keep developing the skills you need and mastering the tasks at hand. Keep believing in yourself and you will eventually achieve your goals.

Top pop vocalist Regina Belle told me that her college music teacher said she should pursue another profession because she could never make it as a professional singer. Today Regina is thankful that she didn't believe him. Like Regina, you can write your own script—and rewrite it again and again if you choose.

Believe that you are capable of creating the life you want for yourself, because you are. You were born for this hour, born to win in life, not to lose. But to be a winner, you need a winner's

attitude. *Get used to thinking of yourself as a winner and to speaking and acting like one.* You don't have to be arrogant or selfish to be your own admirer. Should you expect anyone to honor you or encourage you more than you do yourself?

Renew your faith in yourself and in your oneness with God. Most people don't live their dreams because they don't believe in their ability to make dreams a reality. When you don't believe in yourself, you don't plan or act to achieve anything great. Life is God's great gift to you. What you do with your life is your gift to God. There is nothing that you want that is too good to be true—believe it!

There's Magic in Believing

The people we most admire, the great achievers, the geniuses, are those who are passionate about their purpose and who believe that life offers unlimited possibilities. These rare individuals don't limit their talent or ingenuity. They use their inventiveness, an attribute that remains virtually dormant in most people but is available to each of us in equal measure. Throughout history, people who have made a difference in the world have known that there is magic in believing.

In 1792 Toussaint L'Ouveture led revolting enslaved Africans to freedom and created Haiti, the first free Black nation in the Western Hemisphere. The Black soldiers were victorious because they believed they were made invincible by the spiritual force of Voodoo, the religion derived from our West African Vodun and Yoruba practices. Their belief empowered them to drive the English, Spanish and finally the French armies into the sea, sending hope of liberation to Africans enslaved throughout the Americas.

When Mary McLeod Bethune arrived in Daytona Beach, Florida, she was a 28-year-old widowed mother with little

money and a big dream. She wanted to build a school for Black girls. "It is in my mind and in my soul," she often said. For Mrs. Bethune, life was an adventure. She believed that all good things are possible with "faith, prayer and endless toil." So she ventured forth and found an empty shack, gathered broken furniture and crates from around town and sold her famously delicious sweet-potato pies to help pay the $11 monthly rent. Mrs. Bethune opened her school on October 3, 1904, with six students—five little girls and her five-year old son, Albert. Her motto was always written on the school blackboard: "Be an artist in all you do." And she was. Within two years enrollment had mushroomed to 250 students, and Mrs. Bethune decided it was time to build a school. She put a five-dollar deposit on land that was the city dump and began orchestrating an ingenious fundraising drive to pay for it. She named the school's first new building Faith Hall. Today that little school is the esteemed Bethune-Cookman College, located on a sprawling 52 acres with eight satellite sites and still growing.

There are endless numbers of people who, with faith and persistence, in harder and harsher times than these, lived their dreams. Although Madame C.J. Walker could neither read nor write, she followed a vision she believed God gave her of creating beauty products for Black women, and she became the first self-made female millionaire in America. By 1916 Sarah Walker had her own manufacturing plant and employed 20,000 people throughout the United States, the Caribbean and Central America.

Deeply impressed and motivated by his own mother's religious faith, by 1920 Marcus Garvey had created the largest and most successful mass movement of Black people in history. The Universal Negro Improvement Association was created with the mission to unite "all the Negro peoples of the world into one great body to establish a country and Government absolutely their own." Under Garvey's leadership the UNIA offered food, housing and jobs to the poor. The organization bought a fleet of steamships and linked millions of Africans throughout the world—in the United States, the Caribbean, South and Central America, Europe and the Motherland. The Jamaican-born Garvey's theology was centered in the Black traditional belief that "God helps those who help themselves."

Ella Baker, the major organizer of the Student Non-Violent Coordinating Committee, which sparked the Black Power Movement, and both civil- and human-rights activists Martin Luther King, Jr., and Malcolm X believed that Black people could liberate themselves. They dedicated their lives to that mission, paving our way. Nobel and Pulitzer Prize–winning author Toni Morrison, entrepreneur and TV talk-show host and producer Oprah Winfrey, and trailblazing filmmaker Spike Lee —they are each living their dreams because they dare to have them and have put their energy behind them.

As the lives of these remarkable women and men show, we can dream and build a world. Or, as is more often the case, we can exist without a vision, without a belief in our ability and the infinite possibilities life offers us. Then we never realize our full potential.

We create our own possibilities through the greatest of God's many gifts to us: a conscious mind that is able to make choices. We have the ability to think critically, make decisions, and act. God gave each of us free will. Our will, our mind, is our power.

Choosing is our major function in life. We are making choices all the time. When we choose not to face our fears and work through them, we give up our power. Fear of any kind, including fear of failing—or succeeding—can be paralyzing. It's impossible to succeed if we are unwilling to change. We may choose to live with the hardships of recurring health, family, money or work problems even though we can choose to change the negative behavior that is causing them. But most

51 ■

often it's a lack of self-esteem—simply not accepting or believing in ourselves—and our resulting depression that limit our world. We human beings are adaptable; too often we accept the pain of living life at half-measure.

But God is so good. We don't have to suffer. We can choose, we can change. First, we must stop negatively comparing ourselves with achievers and believing they've been given an advantage and have something special that we lack. Each of us must believe that life offers us infinite possibilities and then choose to do the work necessary to develop into a person we'll admire. The difference between achievers and folks stuck in the mud? Achievers make time for critical thinking, then they plan and execute.

Everything that is knowable you can learn—if you dedicate yourself to acquiring the knowledge or skill. There is no dream too big to make real, no problem too complex to solve. We possess a precious and awesome power. And it's absolute.

It *is* possible to learn any language, science or technology; it is possible to have your best body, do fulfilling work, travel the world. We *should* have the divine-right relationships, be happy, healthy and wealthy. We *can* feed the hungry, house the homeless, restore order in our communities and create peace in the world. We have the power—and the responsibility—to participate fully in life. In our elder years we don't want to look back regretting that we let life pass us by or that we were the first generation who didn't move the race forward. It *is* possible to dismantle oppressive social structures and institutions. But while most of us pay lip service to the struggle against racism, sexism and greed, there are people whose time and energy are focused on preserving and promoting the status quo.

Take courage and liberate yourself. Begin rejecting any limiting thoughts that are undermining your self-esteem and success. No one can give you a positive self-image. This is work that only you can do. Let's face it, we all have personal issues to address. To take charge of your life, you must have the courage to look at yourself honestly.

Spirit speaks to us in many ways. Discomfort or discontent in any area of your life is a call from God to examine that aspect of yourself. Anything that is keeping you from your happiness can be overcome with information, dedication, compassion and patience. You must try to comprehend and make every effort to discover the limitless power within you.

Whatever you believe about yourself, and what is possible for you to achieve, is true. If you believe that you can succeed in life, you are right. If you believe that your life is overwhelming, again you are right. We create the life that supports our internal image of ourselves. We create our own possibilities and impossibilities.

All that humankind has created down through the ages shows that human beings are capable of doing wondrous things. Your great challenge is to believe this about yourself. That belief and courage can only be established inwardly. God created us with the power to create—to create lives of our choosing. To doubt ourselves is to doubt the power and intelligence of God. We are one with God, and we can never be separated from our divinity in any way. The ultimate purpose of life is to accept the truth of our divinity and grow in the awareness of it. Hold on to the truth that you are human and divine, that you can realize your dreams, that life offers you infinite possibilities. Armed with that faith, like the awesome women and men who've achieved great things, you, too, will venture forth and create a life so fulfilling you will hardly be able to wait for each day to begin.

53 ■

WISDOM OF THE SPIRIT

There is a wisdom that is as much a part of our being as our flesh and blood and bones: intuition, the deepest knowing. It is alive in us as children as simple faith in our feelings. But as we grow up and the outer world begins to matter more, the channel to intuition narrows. Western culture stifles intuition, dismissing what can't be explained logically and scientifically, and discouraging reflection and feeling. It offers no real answers to how life should be lived. But life is more than the physical, biological and mechanical—more than what we can see and prove.

Intuition is a higher form of mind than rational thinking. It's the synthesis of the heart, mind and soul working to expand awareness and understanding. Intuition is the wisdom of the Spirit within us, coaxing us to be fair, to do the right thing, to embrace change as a natural and essential part of life. Intuition is the voice within that is forever pressing us to stretch ourselves, to take risks, to keep loving and giving birth to a new self.

Trusting the inner voice is a particular struggle for women.

Sexist oppression has inculcated in us the belief that our thoughts and feelings are only marginally relevant. Our voices are rarely encouraged, our ideas are repeatedly shunned. Part of our work as sisters and brothers must be to honor ourselves and correct the historic devaluation of Black womanhood. One of the ways we affirm ourselves is by listening inwardly and defining for ourselves what it means to be a citizen of the world, what it means to be a human being, a person of African heritage, a descendent of those who were the first people God created.

The recognition and affirmation of our intrinsic beauty, richness and grace are a particular necessity for women. That is the truth of who we are, the truth within us, the truth that the world teaches us to forget. Listening to yourself is critical to your self-esteem and plays the pivotal role in embracing your value and worth.

How do we train ourselves to listen inwardly? How do we relearn the language of the soul? Spirit is always orchestrating our lives and guiding us. But to decode its messages we have to dismiss negativity and fear. *We have to close the door on the chaos of the world. Listening in silence helps us to experience Spirit.*

Truth can come in a flash. More often it unfolds over time. We are always spiraling onward and upward, always moving toward the Divine. No matter what difficulty we are facing, we must never despair but must hold fast to the truth that we are growing. Even when we feel we are losing ground, we are gaining. When it seems otherwise, it's only our misperception and our inability to see the bigger picture.

Life is change. To resist change is to work against the flow of life rather than surrender to and trust it. The essence of life is the journey—the events, conditions, experiences that mold and shape us and at times knock us about. Life is not the arrival at the destination, but the getting there, the process of moving forward that invariably includes leaping and stumbling, soaring and diving, getting soot in your eye and feeling the warmth of the sun on your face. Life is a challenge. That's God's plan. It's our challenges that make us turn inward. Without challenges, we would never know the power and the wisdom of Spirit.

We know how Spirit speaks to us. When we listen and act, balance is restored in our lives. Looking inward, growing in awareness of our oneness with God and learning from Spirit is the purpose of life. If you take quiet time, time to listen to the wisdom of the Holy Spirit, it will guide and protect you. It will never fail you, not once in your life.

T*RANS-*
FORMATION

No matter how tangled your life may seem, no matter how great the loss you've experienced or how deep the rut you're in, like Dr. Marie Jackson-Randolph, you have the capacity to transform yourself and bring forth a new beginning. While we've all had our challenges and been through our changes, few of us have had our sanity and strength tested to the degree that she has. In all the years that *Essence* has been documenting Black women's life experiences, none has touched me more deeply or inspired me more than Bebe Moore Campbell's story about this Detroit-based sister who climbed back from the edge.

As a young mother, Marie Jackson lived through every parent's nightmare: Her baby girl died of sudden infant death syndrome. Several years later, when Marie was a divorced mother of three and battling Boeck's sarcoid, a blood cancer, which was in remission, tragedy struck again. She was working at three jobs, trying to maintain the lifestyle her children had enjoyed before she became a single mother: She was president of a business college and teaching at a community college and

had recently opened Sleepy Hollow, a 24-hour day-care center to help overworked parents like herself.

"The thing about it, the thing about that day," Marie said of May 9, 1979, "is that it was so ordinary." Her girls, Candy, 11, and Tiffany, 7, had returned from getting their hair cornrowed. That evening they taught their mother how to do cartwheels, and Marie took a spin on Candy's new bike before fixing dinner. Today Marie believes that Michael, her 18-year-old son, had a premonition. When he arrived home late for dinner, he said he was delayed because he wanted to say good-bye to his friends.

While all of Marie's children excelled academically, Michael was a scholar. He had entered Tougaloo College at 15 as a math and science major and was about to graduate from Wayne State University's combined bachelor- and master's-degree program. That muggy May evening Michael wanted to turn on the air conditioner to cool the house off. His mother reminded him that the electrician was still working on some wiring and had cautioned them not to use the air conditioner or the pinball machine. Michael didn't listen.

At about 11:30 P.M., Marie was shaken awake from a half sleep by her daughters' cries that there was a fire in the house. Marie was dazed. She stumbled out of bed. When she opened the door to the basement, the intensity of the heat scorched her upper body. Marie reached for the phone, but there was no dial tone. As Bebe wrote, "Dazed and confused, believing the fire was contained in the basement, she reasoned it would take her a split second to rush to a neighbor's house and call the fire department before the danger increased. But during the few moments she was gone, the alcohol in the basement bar caused an explosion and the entire house filled with smoke; her children were trapped."

Marie watched in horror as Tiffany's and Michael's bodies were carried out of the house, their faces covered with sheets.

Later that night Candy died in the hospital. During my recent conversation with Marie, she recalled, "That was the day that the earth and my life stood still. The nurses had to tie me to the bed." Her former husband accused her of killing their children. A local newspaper lambasted her, calling her a negligent mother. Somehow she lived through her children's funeral. Breakdowns, hospitalization and a suicide attempt followed. The cancer flared up again, but she refused to take chemotherapy. Marie wanted to die.

But she didn't die. She finally got up and began rebuilding her life. Today she says in retrospect, "God took everything that was important to me." For years Marie questioned herself and questioned God, until she simply got tired of questioning. Her only consolation today is that she believes her loss was part of God's divine plan. "God humbles us in order to uplift us," says Marie. "I think I have suffered so that I could be an instrument. I have dedicated my life to advocating for children. I lost my four children, but through my work I've been a surrogate mother to about 8,000."

In the years since the fire, Marie's Sleepy Hollow day-care center has grown from one to 16 nurseries, 13 of which are open seven days a week, 24 hours a day. "I cherish the memory of my children through the little ones I care for. Had my own lived, I would not be as committed to helping other children," Marie says.

While Marie doesn't expect ever to stop aching for her children, she says, "I am grateful to God that I got out of the bed of self-pity and have the courage to stand straight and tall. Every time I'm ready to give up again, I remember the James Cleveland song 'If You Can Hold Out Until Tomorrow.' The promise of these children's tomorrow serves as the catalyst for my tomorrow." Marie encourages, "Whether you are out of a

job, ill, alone or struggling with an addiction, you simply have to fight anyway."

Near the end of our talk Marie told me that surviving her tremendous loss has given her the courage and faith to overcome any challenge. Serenely and simply she says, "Life is a game, and you have to master it. Life requires strength."

Dr. Marie Jackson-Randolph remarried and returned to school and is now a practicing attorney—and her cancer is in remission. She built the largest Black-owned chain of 24-hour day-care centers in the country and, with her husband, Thomas H. Randolph, founded the Jackson-Randolph School of Achievement for children in kindergarten through eighth grade. Marie Jackson-Randolph's life is confirmation that unimaginable pain and suffering can lead to transformation, and that with Divine Understanding even the greatest anguish can propel us toward positive action.

Talk to God. And listen inwardly. There is no burden too large or too small to take to the wisdom of the Spirit. No matter how painful or shameful the ordeal or the level of fury or hostility you feel, once you take the problem to God the healing begins. The door is always open. The sweet Spirit resides in you for this purpose: to lift you above the difficulties on the physical plane, to comfort and restore you, to give you insight and wisdom. We give positive value to traumatic experiences by asking the Mystic within, *How can this difficulty enlighten and strengthen me and make me an even better person?*

Wherever we are in life is the perfect starting point—it's the *only* starting point—for moving our lives forward. Even from the depths of despair we are capable of renewing ourselves and making a fresh start. This is the single fact that I appreciate most about life.

While we cannot change the past, with the wisdom of Spirit we can change what it means to us and to our future. With understanding and compassion, we can break a cycle of despair, rise above our sorrows and find a new emotional home from which to create a brighter tomorrow. Each breath we take offers us another chance to create a better life. We have the power of God within us, the power to transform ourselves—a power that is realized by fully living the present moment.

Trans-formation

63 ■

You ARE LOVE

Loving is our strongest human need. In our effort to satisfy our deepest craving, we regularly look outside ourselves to find a person to love. Don't you love being in love? I know I do. I've invested more time and energy in love relationships than I have in most other things. But a relationship with another person will never satisfy our hunger for love.

You can build a life with another person, you can share heart to heart. But making someone other than yourself responsible for your personal fulfillment places an unfair burden on that person. It assigns a task to someone else that is yours alone. We'll never feel content if our happiness depends on someone else's behavior. Expecting another person to get inside our head and to meet our various unspoken needs encourages us to be manipulative and sets us up for certain dissatisfaction and disappointment.

Do you know yourself? Do you know the difference between your needs and the things your ego demands to mask your fears and insecurities? It takes much soul-searching to discover what is true for you, what in life is important, what your own

values are as opposed to those imposed upon you or those you've adopted out of convention.

Looking to our relationships for our love is like looking outside ourselves for a lifeline. It's also putting the cart before the horse. Until we discover love within ourselves, we can't authentically share it with anyone else.

We confuse the rush of romance for love and give it more weight than it deserves. We give great importance to the symbols that Hollywood has assigned to love—good looks, great sex, an air of success and certain refinements. We are all attracted by them. We're often entrapped by them. But these are gorgeous accessories, not the basis for building a solid, lasting relationship. They have no connection to love because they don't sustain us or satisfy us over time.

Love is everlasting. Love is the activity of life, the active power in all of creation, present everywhere, at every moment, in exactly the same degree. We are sustained by love and couldn't separate ourselves from it even if we tried. Love binds us to God, to one another, yet allows us individuality at the same time. A loving relationship is a delicious thing, but it's not where love begins. A romantic relationship provides us with an opportunity to express love, but with or without a relationship, love exists in us and as us.

Love. We think about it, speak about it, celebrate it in song and dance. But we must move beyond the many clichés and abstract ways in which we refer to love. The great spiritual teacher Eric Butterworth, who has informed much of my thinking over the years, says we must personalize and practice what it means to be created in the image and likeness of God. He says we should "Note the logical implication of this. Each of us is created in and of love. God loves us. God is love in us. Each of us is the very activity of love. We have all the love we need to love everyone and everything."

Our joy and happiness depend on our willingness to draw a

larger circle of love, to love one another, as God loves us, without motives or conditions. For us to achieve this ideal means making a basic choice: to focus on love and let go of the rest. To begin seeing each person through the eyes of God.

This might be more easily done in some idyllic place away from the push and pull of everyday life. But for us to maintain a consciousness of love, we must make a constant effort. Meditating on love daily will help you stay centered in the flow of love: Allow your eyes to close. Take a few deep breaths. Now relax your breathing, and let it find its own natural rhythm. As you exhale, feel yourself descending deeper and deeper within yourself. When you feel completely relaxed, imagine you're as light as a feather, floating through the air to a favorite quiet spot—a field of fragrant flowers, the shore of a crystal lake, the gentle slope of a grassy hill. Feel yourself resting here. You feel so free, so safe, at one with the love and beauty surrounding you, the perfection that *is* you.

Talk to God within you. Ask for the strength to love and for help in releasing anything from your heart that is not an expression of love. Feel the healing energy moving through your body, sweeping away any fear, anger, jealousy—any negativity you are holding. Anything that is not in harmony with love is releasing itself from you, floating away, and you smile as it leaves you. Feel the loving energy bubbling up inside you, streaming out of your every pore into the universe and back into you. You feel so good, so peaceful: Your heart is open.

Loving requires openheartedness and the moral courage Dr. Martin Luther King, Jr., so often spoke of. It requires that we make a fundamental choice to act with kindness and charity and that we begin reorganizing our thinking and our lives in ways that are consistent with our choice to be loving.

We must take time to think about what choosing to be loving really means in our lives. Dr. King said that after much contemplation he felt he had discovered for himself the most durable

power in the universe and "the highest good. It is love." Love was the guiding principle in his life. Even as a young man in his twenties, with most of his life still before him, his commitment to love gave him the courage to risk life and limb for the freedom of his people. His commitment to love gave him the courage and conviction to do what he felt was God's will. While we may not make the enormous personal sacrifices that Dr. King made, we, too, must search our soul to discover what choosing to love will mean in our lives.

What will the decision to be loving require when your parents or your partner get on your last nerve? How will you behave when faced with a great disappointment? How will you respond when someone disrespects you, treats you unfairly or unkindly? Will you say within yourself to the person who hurt you most in your life I *love you*, I *forgive you and* I *bless you*? Will you forgive yourself in exactly the same way?

Patience, kindness and gentleness are among the greatest virtues, but sometimes we believe they are signs of weakness. Just the opposite is true. It takes great strength to love someone who has been unlovable. If you are having difficulty in any relationship, you can take the first step in changing the energy between you and the other person. You can send blessings to anyone you find hard to love.

Make a list of the person's good qualities—everyone has good qualities—and bless the person for those good things. Say within yourself I *bless you for your intellect, your neatness* or whatever it is you admire. Say it from your heart and mean it. Then think about the person's behavior that you don't like— maybe it's selfishness and negativity. Turn the paper over and make a list of the traits that are the opposite of the disruptive behavior—in this case, generosity and positiveness. Now bless the individual in the same way for possessing those good qualities.

Sending your blessings a few times a day to a person you are in conflict with is helpful in reducing misunderstanding and hostility: It doesn't change the other person; it changes you. It softens your heart; it helps how you treat and respond to that person. When you resent or resist someone, that negativity is felt by them just as your openheartedness is.

No matter how horrible someone's attitude may be, negativity is diminished in the light of love. Relate to what's best about troublesome people. This way we encourage them to magnify their good qualities and help them to grow. During your conversations, sincerely try to substitute praise for condemnation. All of us—regardless of how we behave or the face we show the world—are yearning for love.

It's no fun holding grudges. The longer you hold on to anger, the more it hardens your heart. Bitterness limits you—your energy and your happiness. When you give up feelings of resentment, you gain inner peace. Loving is essential to your own spiritual development.

When you make the choice to love without condition, you feel closer to the people in your world and there is less tension and stress in your life. You are living on higher ground.

Love is a magnet; it attracts the best of everything. It attracts the most positive relationships, because nothing less will do. When you are a loving person, you don't have to look for meaningful relationships. People are drawn to you because you are nonjudgmental: They can be themselves with you, so they want to be in your loving space.

When you open your heart, you are ready for communion and your lovemate appears. You aren't looking for perfection. You see a relationship as a chance for both you and your partner to unfold and develop. When you are loving, you are doing God's work. You are living the truth of your being; you're in perfect balance, so you feel strong and secure. You've come to the relationship with a full cup. You have love bubbling up inside you, so you're not needy, not looking for your partner to

give you what you are giving yourself. Your honey's love adds sweetness to an already satisfying life. Loving gives you grace and divine understanding. You love your partner despite any faults—because you love yourself in spite of your own.

Trust that everything you need can be gained through loving. Like tuning in to music on your radio, you don't have to understand radio waves in order for it to work. You only have to plug it in and turn it on.

Discovering the nature and power of love must become our life's work. Our people and the many suffering throughout the world are counting on our awakening. Love and peace are possible through our example. We can only grow in our understanding of the divine process by putting it into moment-to-moment practice. Don't wait for love: You *are* love. Get busy loving. Loving gives you the inner peace and freedom you are seeking. Loving gives you wings.

SOUL
TO
SOUL

For years I'd said it: If I ever marry again, I'll bring my best self to that sacred union. And I really believed I would. After all, I was just out of my teens the first time I married, and neither Billy nor I had a clue as to how to make a marriage work. And so ours didn't. Still, it was one of the most valuable experiences of my life. I learned that neither partner wins an argument, and that hurling harsh words can cause both parties tremendous pain and do irreparable damage. I became a mother, and through that experience I learned more discipline and more about the challenge of giving unconditional love. I learned to value patience and kindness. I learned that a relationship can't *make* you happy, that you must bring your happiness with you. And for the many years that I was single, special relationships taught me invaluable lessons: The brothers in my life have been my teachers—and my students.

I *have* remarried, and although I know more about life and love and what it takes to make a relationship succeed, I still have lots of inner work to do. I still have some distance to travel

71 ■

before meeting my best self. Our intimate relationships hold a mirror before us, exposing a self we don't often see. Here is where the personal issues we've not resolved become visible. We easily observe flaws and faults in others, but find looking at ourselves honestly difficult to do.

I have all intentions of being my highest self in all of my interactions, but achieving that for even a day is difficult to do. Surely I brought the better parts of me—a generous spirit, a curious mind, a capacity for compassion and tenderness, and a love for childlike fun—to this marriage to Khephra. But I also brought along a lifetime of ingrained habits and fixed opinions and personal insecurities. When I'm brave enough to look at these, I see how they distort my perception, influence my behavior and ultimately make me unhappy.

Loving is letting go. Letting go of the need to judge and the need to control. It's taming our demands, making them preferences. It's being easy with ourselves and with our partners and letting our relationships flow. It's encouraging our partners to be themselves, to grow and develop in their own time and their own unique way. Intellectually, we know this. *Living* lovingly is the challenge.

Our intimate relationships offer us the greatest opportunities for self-discovery and personal growth—these emotionally charged unions bring forth our best selves as well as reveal the things we need to change. To increase our happiness and the quality of our relationships, we must be honest in examining our behavior and our partnerships. We must ask ourselves if our relationships are working and if they are healthy and constructive. If not, why not? Have we become complacent, or too demanding? Are we giving what we want to receive? Are we settling for less than we deserve? The answers lie within. We need only listen so we can begin making positive changes moment to moment.

The spiritual purpose of our partnerships is to help us break through the walls of our separateness. Loving is an exercise in sharing and accepting—ourselves and one another. It's risking a journey of self-revelation together, soul to soul.

INTIMACY BINDS US HEART TO HEART

One of the greatest expressions of love and support that we sisters and brothers can give one another is the encouragement to be ourselves and to speak honestly and freely in our love relationships.

Remember being a child and tucking away the thoughts and feelings you believed would displease the adults around you? We didn't ask all our questions, express all our feelings or always tell the truth. Early on we learned to make secrecy sacred and that it's safer to wear the mask.

Now, as adults, many of us are living in quiet desperation, suppressing our inner voices and never sharing our truest selves. We continue the practice of restraining valid needs, important instincts and vital parts of our histories because we fear disapproval or outright rejection. But it is crucial to our feelings of self-worth that we affirm ourselves by accepting and being ourselves. Otherwise we never live fully or freely, we never release what Eric Butterworth calls our "imprisoned splendor."

Racism makes our relationships the most vulnerable. It drains so much of our energy, and it puts tremendous emo-

tional and economic pressures on Black love. Because there are few places where we sisters and brothers feel safe expressing ourselves fully, our home front must be safe harbor, the place where introspection and honest self-expression are encouraged. More love, more respect, more understanding—these are the answers to how we can salve any hurts between us. We are striving toward unity in our relationships, not uniformity.

If you feel too self-protective, too afraid to risk being yourself, you can begin developing the courage to be freer with trustworthy people by pressing through the fear. *Within yourself, insist on trusting and being yourself, insist on your essential freedom.* In time you will begin to feel brave and safe. You will begin to bind hearts with others because your freedom to *just be* makes them feel safe to *just be* with you.

The first time I put this to the test was in a love relationship with a man who was a quick wit, smart, fun to be with, but not one who easily shared his emotions. He wouldn't readily speak about his struggle out of a South Bronx housing project through college, then through Columbia University's law and business schools. He didn't speak much about the humiliation I knew he often endured at work.

At the time I was at a crossroads in my life. I was determined that if I was in a love relationship, it had to become intimate before it became sexual—it had to be real. There would be no more pretending with men. No more leaving out chunks of my life because those experiences weren't pretty or exposed my weaknesses and vulnerabilities. I was determined to get comfortable being as open and honest in a love relationship as I was with my closest womenfriends.

This particular evening my new love and I were having dinner in a cozy restaurant near my apartment. We were sitting at a corner table chatting, laughing and exchanging stories when I thought I would chance sharing a deeper part of me. *What incident important to my development would I rather not share with a new love?* I pondered. Well, I certainly had never told a man whom I wanted to love me that another man had been violent toward me. *That's it!* I decided, and I began coaxing myself to share that turning point in my life. But *what if he now sees me as damaged or foolish or simply a woman he doesn't want to invest in loving?* I protested. I had to remind myself that that was the whole point: to trust sharing what is true for me—my important experiences and deepest feelings—and if the brother couldn't handle them or decided he didn't want to be with me, then he wasn't a friend, my divine-right man, and certainly didn't belong in my bed. As I began to speak about the painful relationship, I saw this wonderful brother's eyes grow softer as he reached for my hand. He asked me questions and offered insights into why so many men are abusive to women.

In time, he began to open closed parts of his life to me. The many times he would say "I can't believe I'm telling you this," I knew he was sharing things he had never dared speak about. We shared our hearts before we shared our bodies. We built a solid and meaningful relationship in which both of us grew. Though today both us are happily married to other people, we continue to love and trust each other and to share heart to heart.

The freedom women have been seeking is what many men want for themselves. More and more progressive brothers don't want to be confined to roles because of their gender. Just as being female doesn't mean you want to do all the house-work, make all the sacrifices or play a minor role, being male mustn't demand that you pay all the bills, hold back your tears or always be ready to fight. It isn't possible to have an intimate relationship with someone you are hiding from. Each of us is at a different point in our self-awareness and understanding of

Intimacy Binds Us Heart to Heart

life. Our goal is to try to love one another as God loves us, with a divine love. God's love is unchanging. It supports us whether we are right or wrong, whether we behave lovingly or badly.

We must make the greatest effort to create loving spaces in our relationships where each partner can share his or her truest self as well as mess up and make up without being punished or losing the other's love.

It is possible to be happy with a lover who is not the model person you had in mind. While we shouldn't compromise our standards, we should relax our demands. Our divine-right partners may be fabulous and supportive people but not rock our world in bed. They may be caring and involved parents, but sloppy around the house. We may love and enjoy being with them, but find their families hard to take. We get frustrated by wanting perfection in our lovers and allow the 10 percent that's missing to overshadow the 90 percent that's great. We don't have to like *everything* about our partners to love them.

I decided to see if my own house was in order. One evening I asked my husband, Khephra, if he feels that I treat him kindly, gently. I assumed he would say I'm a real sweetie pie, so I was jolted when he told me that lately I've been critical and short with him. Immediately my mind raced for excuses: I can always find excuses for the stuff I don't want to own. But I reminded myself not to be defensive, and to allow Khephra to share what he was feeling, not just what I wanted to hear. So I opened my heart to the painful truth. Now I'm working at being softer with my honey.

Asking your partner on occasion if any of your behavior is hurtful or annoying puts you in touch with parts of yourself you may need to work on. It will surely go a long way in keeping your relationship openhearted, happy and strong.

Although it's not easy, I'm trying to hold my emotions—and my tongue—in check until I can think of a loving way to respond. And the one who is benefiting most is me. I feel great when I choose not to nitpick or be irritated by someone else's behavior. I'm working on being more tolerant and trying to distinguish people's hearts from their habits and conditioning. That's certainly how I would like to be considered.

Working at our relationships is a sacred task. We should see them as spiritual and political unions, where we practice loving and work toward building the future for our families and our people. We should try to bring a gentle spirit, more progressive thinking and a commitment to critical self-examination to all our interactions. When we are loving, we feel the inner peace and harmony we are striving for. Loving. It's our purpose, it's why we are created. If we are fortunate, we discover that truth and try to live as loving beings before the end of our lives.

Is your house in order? How do you treat your loved ones? We sisters and brothers must create room for disagreement and discussion without slaying one another. We must make every effort to communicate with love and clarity, without bitterness or anger.

When two people can safely share heart to heart, they strengthen their love, their bond. They become friends. Between friends there is truth and trust. Friends *want* to stay together. And in a nurturing and supportive environment our children thrive.

We are alive and can create a positive future for our children because large numbers of Black people committed themselves to one another and to the liberation of the tribe. Despite their differences, and during more difficult times than these, our foreparents loved, worked and built together. Or else we wouldn't be.

Our time on earth is but a moment in our larger history. We should try to get our moment right.

In the Spirit

An Ashanti proverb counsels: *The ruin of a nation begins in the homes of its people.* The commitment to love needed in our community must begin in each of our hearts and homes.

Take Time to Love

Months—even years—go by when we're completely out of touch with folks who've had great meaning in our lives. Often we don't remember the last time we visited that friend who was there for us at a critical moment. Or when we last called that elderly neighbor or family member who always showed us special kindness when we were youngsters. There are people we love dearly who are unaware of our feelings because we don't tell or show them; we don't make room for them in our busy lives. With so much on our expanding agenda we can easily lose sight of the most important things in life: relationships that connect us with ourselves, and with one another.

Today I have fewer personal relationships than I did a decade ago. Though these relationships are deep and meaningful, I now realize that the hurt I experienced in a particular friendship made me overly cautious. I began distancing myself from a few friends who are important to me and not sharing as readily in newer friendships.

Loving takes time; it also requires faith. We build defenses

to protect ourselves from disappointment. But this makes us paranoid and forever on guard. Being defensive is a lot of work and it creates in us a feeling of isolation. Relationships develop through sharing time—and truths.

We need to be our truest self in our friendships. We need to feel the freedom to be "who we be." Free to be lighthearted and silly if the mood strikes us. Free to dance and play and jump at the sun if the spirit moves us. We need to feel free to contradict ourselves, to talk about our insecurities, or not to talk at all. In being our down-to-earth, natural selves, we build bridges that connect us. The success of these connections depends on the safety of the bridges.

We have to choose our friends wisely and never abandon good common sense. Honesty and acceptance never mean becoming anyone's doormat or tolerating disrespect. Inviting a disruptive or destructive person into your life is choosing pain. We have to accept that there are some folks we must love from a distance.

We are at our best when surrounded by happy, healthy people, people who hold a positive vision and who show by their actions that they sincerely like us. People who tell us the truth.

None of us has the time or energy to have ten best friends, given the commitment that true friendship requires. And there are degrees of friendship. In order to grow, we need widening circles of diverse people with whom we can share various parts of ourselves; we need different allies for different things. The person with whom you discuss your most intimate feelings might not be the one to help you invest your money, or the person to give you the best career advice.

A great part of loving ourselves and encouraging personal growth is exposing ourselves to people who challenge us to see new ways of looking at the world. So I don't lose hope, I need to be around people who are working toward social change, folks who are serious about empowering African people. I want to share more with friends who live holistically—they help us to master ourselves and our gifts. I want to interact and share strengths with our youngsters and with people who love art, literature, language—and life. I need more time with my womenfriends and with couples whose love has stood the test of time. I want to spend time with people who love and serve God.

As our lives become ever more hectic, we must regularly reorder our priorities to share with and thank the people who support us—our parents, children, lovers and friends. Tell the folks you admire just how wonderful you think they are.

I had a painful reminder several years ago of how important it is that we let others know how much we care. When top fashion designer Willi Smith died, I wished I had told him more often how much I loved him, how inspired I was by his work. I wished I had looked into his smiling eyes more, hugged him more and shared more of his great humor and joy. I've wondered often since his death how I could have loved him so much without taking time to show it.

Willi was swept away from us so quickly. He was here one day, gone the next. His sudden death reminded me that we never know the moment or the hour that we'll lose someone dear, or when we ourselves will succumb. I addressed the crowd gathered at Willi's memorial, sent flowers to his dear grief-stricken sister, Toukie, but I wish I had given Willi his laurels while he was alive.

I'll always remember the wisdom shared by Sarah Vaughan and Sammy Davis, Jr., during our interviews for the half-hour documentary specials Essence Television produced on each of them. Although I didn't know it at the time, I interviewed both Sammy and Sarah near the end of their lives. They shared similar sentiments. They agreed that they had earned large sums of money and achieved great fame, that they'd been received by kings and queens throughout the world, had ac-

cepted accolades and honors and had lived in the most exquis-ite homes. But when they reflected on their lives, each of them said that over time those things didn't matter much, that those weren't their golden moments. Both Sarah and Sammy said that it was their relationships, the precious time out of the spotlight, the time they shared with family and friends, that had the most meaning and that had given them their greatest re-wards. I always want to remember that.

No matter how busy we are, how closely the world presses around us and how much of our time our schedules seem to demand, we must make time for heart-to-heart sharing. We must take time to love.

BLESSED BE THE FAMILY

When we were children, the family connection was our support system for survival. It was where we learned how to be ourselves and where we learned how to be with others. It was where our thoughts, behavior, ideals and beliefs were formed. Then it was our family's responsibility to nurture and shape us.

When we grow up and something goes awry in our lives, we may look back on our upbringing and find our parents guilty—guilty of being human. It seems no matter how dedicated they were in rearing us, we feel we needed something more, something vital that wasn't provided. Difficulties in relations are a given, and the parent–child connection is the most complex of all. And if truth be told, some of us were raised by unstable people, people suffering from emotional traumas, addictions, anger, grief. As every parent knows, we are raised by people who are grappling with their own personal issues, struggling to order their own lives.

My father, the young Lawrence Taylor, arrived in Harlem from St. Kitts, West Indies, in the early 1920's, dressed in a suit

and tie and ready to do business. By 1937 he had met and married my mother, and together they opened a ladies' clothing store below their apartment in East Harlem. I grew up in that store in the 1950's. My mother became a housewife, and I became my father's little helper. In Daddy's store I learned how to count, make change and keep the merchandise neat. I finally graduated to selling stockings. Daddy and Mr. Williams, the man who sold candles, incense and lucky-number books a few doors down from us, were the only Black entrepreneurs in that thriving area around 116th Street and Park Avenue. All the other stores were owned by Eastern Europeans—"the refugees," as my parents referred to them—who had fled Hitler's army.

Lawrence was a good man. He was smart, stern, confident. He didn't smoke, drink or cuss. He was refined, respectful—the kind of man who tipped his hat in the presence of women. He supported his family, and he came home every night after he closed his store. I don't remember my mother or us children ever wondering where Daddy was. We always knew. His world was small—he was either running his business or at home. But while the family had the benefits of his physical presence and financial support, emotionally he was miles away. Lawrence was a quiet, sullen man whom I never once saw hug anyone. I took his sadness personally. I thought he didn't like me.

During my younger years I longed for a closer relationship with my father, and as I grew older, I tried to fashion it. Even after I'd moved away from home, when I visited my family I'd curl up on Daddy's lap, despite his protests. I'd kiss his bristly face, then force his lips to my cheek and insist on my kiss ("One I can hear, Daddy") before I'd let him alone.

It wasn't until a decade after my father died that I began to understand his pain. Then I could see he'd spent most of his life trying to keep his cool, that his silence was a coping mechanism, his retreat from the daily insults and psychological hurts he endured in a racist America, where his manhood was being systematically destroyed. His sullenness was one of the many layers of armor that shielded his heart, that helped him deal with living without the full privileges of manhood.

We could spend a lot of time recounting the things that went wrong in our childhood. We were reared by people laboring on so many levels, trying to make sense of their lives, struggling for their families to survive. It's no surprise that some of what they passed on to us may be less than positive.

Those of us who've been told that we're lucky to have been reared in two-parent households may have suffered in the cross fire of our parents' conflicts. Others were reared by single parents saddled with being mother, father, breadwinner—and who may have felt overwhelmed and unfulfilled.

After sharing painful childhood experiences with people whose parents died or abandoned them when they were children, you feel blessed even if living with yours was a struggle. There are so many among us who were raised by uncaring surrogate parents or in cold, impersonal institutions where they never felt wanted or that they quite belonged. I can tell you that even the most hurtful things parents do are seen in a gentler light after they are gone. And trying to heal a relationship across an abyss of death is infinitely more difficult than extending a healing hand to our parents while they are here.

Whatever our parents' experiences, we can be assured they operated in an often hostile environment, where their challenges were greater than our personal needs. Yes, I wished my father would have hugged me and kissed me. That he could have expressed his love the way I felt I needed it. And had talked to me rather than trying to teach me with intimidation and whippings. Until I began to understand the many pressures he withstood for our family's survival, I believed he didn't

love me. If I hadn't moved past me, me, me, I might never have tried to understand his pain and might have been inhibited from expressing love as I matured.

My father was Victorian, born on a little Caribbean island in 1898. He didn't have his first child until he was in his mid-forties. Nothing in his experience could have prepared him to raise a vocal, adventurous girlchild coming of age in New York City during the freedom-loving sixties.

Once I began to investigate my father's life, his upbringing, his relationship with his parents, I could see why he was uneasy with any show of tenderness, and that he was simply treating me the way his parents had treated him. Then I stopped waiting on his affection. I stopped taking his behavior personally. I did the hugging. And the touching. I learned not to wait on love, but to get busy giving it.

Even if we cannot help a parent change hurtful behavior, we don't have to continue to feel beaten down by it. We don't have to keep it alive in us by inviting experiences into our adult lives that recreate our childhood pain. The more you hold on to the painful past, the less you can experience the joy of this moment. When we feel stuck in some area of our lives, it's often because we have some forgiving to do.

There is no one whose life is more closely woven into yours than your mother's—even if she was absent during your childhood or seemed distant, as mine did. Although my mother's life revolved around her family and she took great care of us, I didn't grow up feeling her warmth. It wasn't in her eyes, in her voice, in her touch. Like Daddy, Mommy seemed uncomfortable with intimacy or displays of affection. That left few channels through which we could connect.

My only memory of being in my mother's embrace was when my first marriage was coming to a volatile end and, clutching my infant daughter to my breast, I took refuge in my parents' home. Mommy greeted me at the door that cold gray winter evening and just that once she opened her arms and encircled the woolen bundles of me and little Shana-Nequai. I'll always cherish that moment, the softness in her eyes, that quick embrace that said, "Welcome home, Susan. I understand."

We've been taught that if as children we are given love, we will grow into loving adults. We've also been taught that if love and affection are withheld, our ability to love will be stifled. Some analysts attribute much of what is or isn't happening in our lives to our relationship with our parents. There is obviously great truth in that because—for all of us—this is our first human bonding. But often society holds to the common notion that our mothers are to be blamed for everything that goes wrong in our lives. We blame them for not protecting us or for protecting us too much; for staying when we feel they should have left, for leaving when we feel they should have stayed; for being too domineering, for being too passive. I find this particularly true when sharing with White folks, especially White women. It's much more difficult for Black folks to blame our mothers, who've been long-suffering and whose backs were always bent doing their work. Yet at times mothers become everyone's scapegoat. We should bless them and relieve them of carrying so much weight.

We must honor the spirit of "motherlove," the nurturing spirit that seeks to promote and protect life and that is not the exclusive responsibility of women. It's an attribute that needs encouraging in every human being; it's the nourishment that's sorely needed in the world today. Motherlove is the caring spirit that compelled my mother to put cardboard in her shoes so her children wouldn't have to. Motherlove inspired our elders to press on, to persevere. Motherlove is unfailing love. Tough stuff. It never gives up.

The spirit of motherlove is central to our African family code, which insists on preserving the clan because it provides the

continuity of culture, tradition and each family member's connection to all of life. Unlike in the West, the African view of self is contingent upon the existence of others. Each family member owes her or his existence to all other members, living or dead or yet to be born. We Africans throughout the diaspora must guard against any further ruin or debasement of the traditional African values that helped us to survive these 400 years away from our homeland. *Motherlove is forgiving and understanding. It longs to heal whatever is fractured.* Because I didn't receive the hugs and kisses I craved as a youngster, when I became a mother I was determined to shower my daughter with affection. I did—still do. I cherish those years when Shana was growing up and we did so many wonderful things together. The trips we took. Teaching her to roller-skate in Central Park. Our evening walks, her shoulder snuggled under my arm as she hugged my waist. The many nights she would crawl into my bed, curl her little body into mine and nuzzle as close as she could get.

But those are my memories, not the ones she always focuses on. Shana says she was often lonely being a latchkey child, that I devoted too much time to the magazine and not enough to her. Now she's a young woman and says I try to control too much of her life, that I have aspirations for her that are not what she wants for herself.

To discover our own "personhood," we must challenge the values of those who shaped us. But often we feel angry at our families for denying us or abusing us in some way and feel that our lives will never be happy because of it. Holding on to the painful past brings the pain forward to the present and projects it into the future, so try blessing it and releasing it.

Painful family issues keep cropping up until we put them in their proper place. Whatever our experience with our parents was, they gave us their best—the best they had within them to give to us at the time. Now we must take the best of what they gave us and weave it into the best within ourselves. We must put together our own life plan, one that fits who we are and who we wish to become. We must work to turn any disappointments of the past into personal power.

Yes, there is much for us to forgive our parents for. I know. I'm a parent. I hope my daughter will be as generous in forgiving her parents as I've tried to be in forgiving my own.

How we do or do not get along with our nuclear and extended families depends not only on them but on us, on how we perceive their actions, how we act and react and judge their behavior. But mostly it has to do with the relationship we build with ourselves. Once we take honest inventory of ourselves and make the primary relationship we have with ourselves a wholesome one, understanding our families will be easier. When our family business is right, we respect our old and nourish our young. We treat each other with grace, compassion and dignity. We accept that we are each other's keeper.

GOING
THE
DISTANCE

A young woman I knew casually was having problems and wanted to talk with me about the sense of hopelessness she was feeling. Although she'd been going to counseling for several years, she said she was as miserable today as the first time she mustered the courage to walk through the therapist's door. I could see the sadness in her eyes, in her furrowed brow, her bent shoulders. I could feel her torment as she spoke about her life—the emotional and sexual abuse she endured as a youngster, the anger she felt toward her mother, her hunger for a satisfying love relationship.

I listened and empathized with her. I felt a bond developing between us, so I shared my own anxieties and insecurities—that my greatest battle has been an internal one, trying to slay my doubts and fears. And that I, too, have had bouts of depression. She seemed amazed that my life, like hers, has been an emotional struggle. She'd assumed that because I'm considered successful, greet people with a ready smile and talk about the transforming power of God in us, I have it all together.

Like yours, my life is a work in progress. We are here to grow, to develop fully, to learn to live in *all* the rooms in our mansion. If we're not working through something, we're not living. Life can be a struggle, and when we face our difficulties, we learn that we are never struggling alone. It is *because* of our challenges, *because* of our anxieties and depressions that we come to know God.

As I shared with the young sister, the difference in my life today is that now when I feel depressed or anxious I don't try to mask the pain or take off in all directions. And I know how not to linger in a painful place. I take the dilemma to my quiet time—to my bath, to my bed, on a long walk through the trees in a nearby park. I turn to God and ask that the lesson and the blessing in the challenge be revealed. Spirit never fails us. It always reveals a way out.

Stuff happens—whether you are rich or poor, Black or White, centered within yourself or off your path. I was sitting with my husband, Khephra, and my friend Pat Martin in a house high on a mountaintop, away from the stress and strain of the city. It was one of those good times that are all too rare in our lives. We were relaxing, chatting, flipping through magazines, listening to the warm tenor sax of John Coltrane, when a phone call from home shattered my peace. There was trouble in the family. They were fussing and fighting, hurting one another with words, and I was being drawn into it.

With one phone call my tranquillity turned into chaos. But not for long. I'd been doing for myself what I speak about, write about and am trying to make my life practice: I'd been taking quiet time each day, time to listen, time to think, time to replenish my mind and spirit with the nourishment that day-to-day living depletes. Had I been moving fast and feeling stressed, I would have immediately been pulled into the family feud. Instead I paused, thought about it for a moment and realized that I didn't need to make the problem mine, that I could listen without becoming part of the mess.

After I hung up the phone, I never even mentioned the disturbance to Khephra or Pat. I just eased back into the warmth of Coltrane's tenor sax and rejoined the fun and laughter that were my choices that day. But I was struck that afternoon by how fragile our peace of mind is—how in an instant circumstances outside us, things we have no control over, can intrude on our world and turn it upside down.

Life is difficult, often painful. Whether you live in the center of the city or on a mountaintop, no matter where you are or who you are or how fully you know God, trouble will find you. If you don't have difficulties in your life today, tomorrow you surely will. Challenges are a natural part of life: They drive our growth, make us inventive and coax us to explore the expansive rooms of our mansion.

Without question, there are times when life's pressures will knock us down, but when we are centered in God, they don't knock us out. When we are centered in our wholeness and oneness with God, any physical, mental or financial difficulties don't overtake us.

Each and every day we must pause to put on our spiritual armor. Through daily communion we develop a deep and personal relationship with God. Then, even if we lose our material possessions, even if we lose our health or our friends, we won't lose our way.

What occurred to me while the young sister and I were speaking about our lives is that giving up is a luxury Black women have never been able to afford. Even when we stumble, we stumble forward, so that we add to the distance traveled. We learned long ago not to fall backward, because there's usually no one there to catch us. Few sisters can go to their families and say "Take care of me." Most often *we* are the caretakers of family and friends.

A womanfriend who is an award-winning writer—now divorced and in her late forties—wrote in *Essence* about her most profound year of growth. DorisJean Austin's second divorce became final in February of that year. Her mother, to whom she was extremely devoted, died of cancer in August, and in November she, too, was diagnosed with uterine cancer and underwent a radical hysterectomy. DorisJean felt unable to cope with the many changes in her life and turned to alcohol to sedate herself. Her drinking quickly escalated into a daily nightmare, and she was admitted to Bellevue Hospital suffering from severe depression that resulted in a nervous breakdown. When she was released, first from the psychiatric hospital and then from a cancer-research hospital, her health didn't permit her to return to work. She was placed on welfare. DorisJean says that when she had no one to turn to, she turned to God and began the long journey back to recovery.

Today DorisJean has a rewarding career as a writer and teacher. She tells me that that challenging year was the most painful yet the most important one of her life. She says she'd never guessed what reserves of strength and faith were available to her simply by praying and working through whatever God placed next in her path.

Today I'm amazed at her enormous joy. There is such strength in her laughter. DorisJean is an active member of Alcoholics Anonymous and carries her Twelve Step Program into her daily life. I have been blessed to spend quiet time sharing strength and hope with this indomitable sister whose spirit conjures up visions of our ancestral mothers, of survivors like Maya, Oprah and Tina and of all our warrior women who show us by their lives that our choices are limitless.

Sometimes when things fall apart, we forget what reserves are ours. Whenever I doubt that I can go the distance, I remember my mother's life. And her mother's struggle. I remind myself of who we are: a people who refused to die. Despite the horrendous physically and emotionally pain-filled history our forebears endured, they kept the faith, they willed themselves to live. This power is their legacy to us. Like them, we must always lift ourselves up, brush ourselves off and take positive action. All that you need begins with you. All that our race needs begins with us. We *must* move forward—for ourselves and for our people. We haven't come this far not to go the distance.

CHOOSING LONGEVITY

One Sunday I was sitting in Harlem's Abyssinian Baptist Church about half an hour before the 11 o'clock service was to begin. Because time is so precious, arriving before the beginning of service is rare for me. But *Essence* was celebrating an anniversary, and the pastor, the Reverend Calvin Butts, had invited me to speak about it at that Sunday's service and asked me to arrive early. The elderly people were the first to enter the church. I watched them making their way to their seats. What a beautiful parade they were. They came with silver hair and Sunday hats. In suits and ties and in fellowship. They came alone and on one another's arms. Some aided by canes, one by a walker. You could easily see they were in varying states of health. *Which one of them will I be like in my elder years?* I wondered.

Since that Sunday I've asked myself the questions we should ask often: How will I spend my later years? Will I be vital and independent, or will I be bent and feeble? Will I be mentally alert, engaged in life—or watching it from the sidelines? Will I even still *be* here? We all *want* to live healthy lives, but are we

choosing longevity? Do our daily habits support or diminish our chances of aging well?

The generations before us didn't have the lifestyle choices we take for granted. Their lives were defined by hard work. When they were young, Hollywood glamorized smoking and drinking. Managing stress was unheard-of. Our forebears inherited the delicious but unhealthy diets of their parents, and they paid the price. I don't want to suffer the strokes that killed my mother, my grandmother and her mother, or the diabetes that took my father's life. I want to avoid the high blood pressure, the arthritis and heart problems, the kidney and weight problems that limit the joy in so many of our elders' lives.

The lifestyle choices we make now will go a long way in determining if we are mentally alert, physically fit and healthy in the autumn of our lives. When we're young and strong, it's hard to imagine ourselves otherwise: We take good health for granted. But good health is not preserved without constant, conscious effort.

While the larger population in this nation is living longer, the opposite is true for us. In our community, a shorter life span and physical debilitation affect the quality of life for more than just the individual. When we die young or are incapacitated, it means a loss of productivity that might otherwise help move our people forward. It saps the time and energy of those who have to care for us because we didn't care for ourselves. A vast amount of wisdom and life experience is lost to our children and generations to come when we fail ourselves.

We know what it takes to achieve longevity. Couch potatoes don't get there. Neither do folks who overeat or smoke or who drink too much or whose diets are high in fat, sugar or salt. We can act from our power instead of from our weakness anytime we choose. You can be disciplined and committed—and must think of yourself as such. You are not inherently weak or inadequate; you are inherently strong. Your will is your most powerful tool. It's God's mind in you. *"I will" are two of the most powerful words you can utter. Words that were in the beginning. Words through which the Creator created worlds. And all that is and ever shall be is but reverberations and repercussions of that first almighty thunderclap. I WILL. It is both a declaration and a command. It affirms dominion. Take a moment and whisper it to yourself. "I will." Feel the power.* Implicit in the words "I will" are the acknowledgement and affirmation that you have the power to choose. If you have the will to preserve your health, you can develop the will*power* that puts you in charge.

We are the parents of our elder selves. One of the most important decisions we must make at this time in our lives is to be better guardians of our health — for ourselves, for our children and for our race.

Passage

All the spaces that my mother occupied in her home and in my life are empty. Mommy died recently, and if you've experienced the death of a beloved parent, you know the loss I feel—the ache, the feeling of aloneness and the subsequent depression. It seems that no matter how fully our parents may have lived, how old they may be or how much they may be suffering, we are never prepared for them to die. We don't want to let them go. But they are blessed if their children outlive them. That is the natural order of our passage.

The feeling of loss would hit me in waves those first days after my mother died. When I'd think of never seeing her again, of never having another conversation with her, I thought I'd never stop aching or crying. But the pain began to ease as I considered my many blessings.

My siblings and I are blessed to have been raised in a home where traditional African values—decency, respect, responsibility and discipline—were instilled in us, insisted upon. We are fortunate to have been raised by a woman who dedicated her life to her family and who was clear about who she was: She

was her own person. "I love myself more than anybody," Mommy would say with a little chuckle that said you'd better believe it.

My mother was known for her directness more than for her diplomacy. For her, the truth was uncomplicated, it needed to be spoken. And I couldn't always handle it. Throughout my life her words would hurt me, anger me, distance me. But never for long—we always found our way back to each other.

My mother's death is helping me see life more clearly. Every breath is so precious, and the next one isn't guaranteed. We each have a finite number of heartbeats, a finite amount of time. But we have enough heartbeats and enough time to do what is important to our lives. Maintaining our health is important. Securing our financial future is important. Spending time with family and friends, the people we love and have history with, is important. Teaching our children to love and cherish themselves is important. Making peace in our relationships is important—today. Life is today.

Change—releasing the known and embracing the new—is the encompassing theme of our lives. It's important to accept that and to see the inevitable changes not as threats but as opportunities that can deepen our understanding and bring us wisdom and growth.

My mother lived and loved long. She enjoyed good health for all of her elder years, save the months before her death. Moms didn't die prematurely, out of season. She had finished her work. For a long time Babs had been saying she was tired. Eighty-two years is a lot of living.

Still, there are those unanswerable questions: Where did she go? How can I reach her?

I believe that Spirit lives on, that it is immortal, and that we must look to our ancestral spirits to guide us. I catch glimpses of my mother when I look in the mirror. I hear her when I speak. She lives in me. And it is with her strength and the strength of her mother, Rhoda, and her grandmother Susan and all the capable and courageous African women who preceded them that I accept the mantle they decorated so brilliantly, and I promise to wear it well.

Passage

THE TRIUMPH
OF THE
SPIRIT

The Motherland. It beckons me often, and I feel so blessed each time I am able to go. I'd been longing to visit Ghana and Côte d'Ivoire, neighboring countries along the coast of West Africa, where the cold Atlantic waters meet the Gulf of Guinea. West Africa, our distant homeland. The region from which our foreparents, among tens of millions of Africans, were stolen and sold during the Atlantic slave trade. Some historians estimate that as many as 100 million West African people were taken from the continent between 1441 and 1850.

It had been more than a decade since I'd visited that part of the continent when I took the *Essence* fashion and beauty team to Senegal on assignment.

I'd been hoping to return to West Africa. I wanted a better understanding of the political and economic changes taking place. I wanted to experience the people and the culture and to see how *Essence* could play a role in building bridges between Africans and African-Americans. But primarily I wanted to get in touch with the history that most diaspora Africans share: I wanted to visit the slave dungeons—the forts and castles, as

they are called—that dot the West African coastline. I wanted to know more about the odious acts of violence and inhumanity that have been committed against our people. I wanted a deeper understanding of what our ancestors experienced—what they suffered and survived to make our lives possible. I wanted to pay homage to their lives and to give thanks for my own.

It is difficult to comprehend the misery that our ancestors endured and survived. What they overcame makes clear that there is an undiminishable force that supports life. You understand that when you enter the slave dungeons in Ghana. They are damp and dark, some pitch-black. In one, dug ten feet into the earth at Cape Coast, as many as 1,000 males were held at a time. It is a place without ventilation where 100 people would feel crowded. Our ancestors were chained and shackled in those dank tombs, where they were forced to urinate, defecate, eat and sleep for months before being shipped to the Americas.

While in Ghana, I learned that most of the Africans taken into slavery were very young. The children and young adults were captured in the outlying regions and herded to the shore. The curator at Cape Coast reported that millions of these young people died during the long trek from the hinterland to the coastal holding pens. He said they would succumb to heatstroke, hunger and exhaustion from having to walk tens of miles carrying the weight of the irons that bound them.

I wanted to return to West Africa to plant my feet in the sand and linger at the water's edge where our foreparents left behind all their tender connections, all that was dear to their hearts. I wanted to pray at the places where they had walked in shackles to canoes waiting to shuttle them to the slave ships.

During the months in the sweltering ship's belly, hundreds of Africans would lie packed together, huddled spoon-fashion, in their own excrement and vomit, bloodied, sick and unattended. On many of the Atlantic crossings, few of the human cargo survived, and the bodies of the many who died were thrown into the sea. Writer Amiri Baraka says that at the bottom of the Atlantic there is a railroad of bones—that sharks would regularly follow the slave ships because they knew they'd be fed. In the Americas millions more met with early, painful deaths.

The wonder is not that so many perished, but that so many survived. *The survival of our ancestors who lived through the Middle Passage and through the horrors of slavery is a story of the triumph of the spirit, the power of the divine.*

Our past affirms that our future is not at the mercy of outside conditions. That we are our own masters—even when in a weakened state. Throughout our history our belief in the mercy of God and our commitment to mutual love and support have been our self-generating mechanisms.

Like you, I get tired and weary of the struggle and at times feel overwhelmed by my life and by the challenges our people face. But looking back on our foreparents' lives, on how they didn't despair and how they triumphed over immeasurable suffering, helps us put our lives in context and gives us the renewed strength of spirit and resolve we need to keep moving on.

While it is true that these are trying times, we must remember that the most difficult days are behind us. No matter how challenging our lives may seem, life will never be as tough for us as it was for our parents and the preceding generations. We are the most blessed generations of Black people anywhere in the world. We have everything we need to take charge of our lives and to move our people forward.

There is a reason why our story of survival is hardly ever told. We have been taught European history so long, we have forgotten our own. If we were aware of our history, we would forsake any untruths about our weakness or incompleteness. Gaining

a clear and conscious understanding of our past would free us of the self-limiting thinking and behavior that are the residue of more than 400 years of debasement and humiliation. Knowing who we are, knowing from whom we come and what our people lived through, would reawaken our determination and resolve. It would mean the end of Black paralysis.

Had we successfully finished resolving all our personal and collective problems, what would our purpose in life be? Now we must take responsibility for our lives. We must strive toward personal excellence and make sure that our behavior corresponds to our values and the future we want for ourselves and

for our children. Now we must have the courage to champion the policies that will improve the lives of the millions who are at risk. Now we must hold ourselves, one another and our government accountable. We must marry intellectualism and activitism, salvation and liberation.

Included among us is the largest group of educated, affluent people of African ancestry anywhere in the world. We were born for this hour. And we are human and divine. The more we believe in our divinity, the greater will be our inner strength, wisdom and clarity. The deeper our relationship with God, the more fortified we feel to withstand life's many challenges. The more centered we are in God's love, the more courageously we venture forth.

Like our grandparents, we must believe in our divinity and direct our lives from that place of inner conviction and assurance. We must trust in God and the truth of who we are. We must walk by faith and not by sight alone.

On the cover:

Detail of Yoruba robe called *agbada*, a traditional Nigerian garment worn on official occasions by chiefs or dignitaries. This robe was tailored around 1930 from hand-spun and handwoven cotton cloth with native silk embroidery. From the collection of Eric Robertson, Eric Robertson African Arts, New York City.